Better Homes and Garden

step-by-step

ornamental
grasses

Christmas, 2001

Merry Christmas Carol.
May this book on grasses
bring you delight
throughout the year.

Love you
Dad

Peter Loewer

Better Homes and Gardens® Books
Des Moines, Iowa

Better Homes and Gardens® Books
An imprint of Meredith® Books

Step-by-Step Ornamental Grasses
Senior Editor: Marsha Jahns
Production Manager: Douglas Johnston

Vice President and Editorial Director: Elizabeth P. Rice
Executive Editor: Kay Sanders
Art Director: Ernest Shelton
Managing Editor: Christopher Cavanaugh

President, Book Group: Joseph J. Ward
Vice President, Retail Marketing: Jamie L. Martin
Vice President, Direct Marketing: Timothy Jarrell

Meredith Corporation
Chairman of the Executive Committee: E. T. Meredith III
Chairman of the Board and Chief Executive Officer:
    Jack D. Rehm
President and Chief Operating Officer: William T. Kerr

Produced by ROUNDTABLE PRESS, INC.
Directors: Susan E. Meyer, Marsha Melnick
Executive Editor: Amy T. Jonak
Editorial Director: Anne Halpin
Senior Editor: Jane Mintzer Hoffman
Design: Brian Sisco, Susan Evans, Sisco & Evans, New York
Photo Editor: Marisa Bulzone
Assistant Photo Editor: Carol Sattler
Encyclopedia Editor: Henry W. Art and Storey
    Communications, Inc., Pownal, Vermont
Horticultural Consultant: Christine M. Douglas
Copy Editors: Sue Heinemann, Amy K. Hughes
Proofreader: Cathy Peck
Assistant Editor: Alexis Wilson
Step-by-Step Photography: Derek Fell
Garden Plans: Elayne Sears and Storey Communications, Inc.

All of us at Meredith® Books are dedicated to providing you with the information and ideas you need for successful gardening. We guarantee your satisfaction with this book for as long as you own it. If you have any questions, comments, or suggestions, please write to us at:

Meredith® Books, *Garden Books*
Editorial Department, RW206
1716 Locust St.
Des Moines, IA 50309–3023

STEP-BY-STEP

Ornamental Grasses

The World of Grasses

Since the beginning of recorded history, grasses have fed the world. Crops such as corn, wheat, oats, and rice are the basic staples for humans, while hay, corn, and sorghum feed livestock. But only recently have grasses been grown as ornamental plants. As such, they have opened up a whole new world of garden design. • When gardeners realized grasses were beautiful as well as useful, the wide variety of available grasses became a great advantage in landscaping. The grass family, Gramineae, is immense: more than 1,400 species occur naturally in the United States alone. Within this family, color, size, and shape vary enormously, giving grasses great decorative potential. • When grasslike plants such as bamboos, sedges, and rushes are added to the equation, even more combinations are possible. From the huge, 120-foot-high giant bamboo to the tiny dwarf fescue, there is an ornamental grass for every garden.

*T*rue grasses all belong to the botanical family Gramineae, which numbers about 700 genera and more than 7,000 species. There are annual grasses with seeds that germinate, develop into plants, then mature, flower, set seed, and die, all in one spring and summer. And there are perennial grasses that live from year to year, often in the form of creeping plants (like the lawn grasses), but sometimes as huge specimen plants (like the cereal corns or eulalia grasses, *Miscanthus* spp.), or as plants with woody stems, typified by the bamboos, which can tower to heights of 100 feet or more.

The grass stem, known as a culm, is often round and hollow, although some grasses—such as corn and several species that grow in very arid regions—have solid stems. The stem sections are joined by solid joints called nodes. The stems may stand erect, as with wheat and corn, or they may bend at the joints and trail along the surface of the ground, as with the infamous crabgrass.

Grass roots are very fibrous, and several kinds of grasses have roots that will penetrate many feet into the earth. It is this quality that makes grasses so valuable for erosion control—and also makes it so difficult to completely remove an unwanted grass without a lot of hard digging.

The leaves of grasses are called blades and have parallel veins. All grasses belong to the monocotyledons, plants that always begin with one seed leaf. (The seed leaf, or cotyledon, is the first leaf a young plant develops; it usually looks different from the other leaves the plant produces as it grows.)

Not surprisingly in a group as large as the grass family, many species are so attractive that gardeners find them to be very valuable as ornamental plants. Whether because of their distinctive leaf structure,

delicate windblown blossoms, decorative seed heads, or ease of maintenance, ornamental grasses continue to grow in popularity.

Grass blades come in a wide variety of shapes; some are long and pointed, some curve in graceful arcs, and others stick out stiffly like swords.

Not only do grasses come in many shades of green, but there are also grasses in a variety of blues, ranging from light to dark to steely. And there are reds and russets, golds and yellows, and in the fall, endless shades of tan and brown. Grasses offer patterned as well as colored foliage. Among the amazing number of variegations are stripes of white or ivory and dashes of creams and yellows.

Grasses can also add a sense of rhythm and movement to the garden. For example, in the wind, the arching blades of the tall landscape varieties act like ocean waves, billowing and flowing in the garden. On calm days, these grasses are static and sculptural, but in the breeze, their blades sway back and forth, creating abstract patterns and soothing rustling sounds.

Grasses are unusual plants because they don't have large and colorful flowers to reproduce seeds. Instead of having to attract pollinators, grasses are pollinated by wind; they release their pollen into the air, to float from flower to flower on gentle breezes.

There are both annual and perennial ornamental grasses. Although annual grasses are rarely grown for their foliage, their flowers and seeds offer many fascinating varieties of form and color. Some annual grasses dry beautifully and can be enjoyed both in the garden and in the home.

When growing perennial grasses, the gardener's biggest concern is often the final size of the plants. A young plant that you purchase may at first look great outside, below one of the first floor windows. A few

A garden devoted to ornamental grasses reveals a wide variety of shapes, colors, and textures. Here the variegated *manna grass* (Glyceria maxima) *in the foreground contrasts with the red of Japanese blood grass* (Imperata cylindrica *var.* rubra) *and soft green of maiden grass* (Miscanthus sinensis 'Gracillimus'). The subtle washes of color play against the strong vertical lines of the giant reed (Arundo donax) *at the rear.*

The effervescent flowers of fountain grasses bloom far longer than most perennials. In the photo on the opposite page, Pennisetum alopecuroides *is in the foreground with a tender species,* P. setaceum *'Cupreum', to the rear.*

years later, however, it may have grown so large that it blocks the view from inside and darkens the interior most of the day. Check the plant's mature size before you put it in your garden.

Except for some of the more unusual cultivars, all of the annual and perennial grasses are easily grown from seed (see pages 128–129 for some sources).

▼ Grasslike Plants

Sedges and rushes are grasslike plants from the family Cyperaceae and are often considered to be grasses because of both their flowers and their leaf structure. On closer examination, however, you'll see they have triangular rather than rounded stems, which are not hollow but have a pithy center. Although not as popular as true grasses, a surprising number of sedges make ideal garden perennials, especially if you are looking for mostly evergreen foliage that is often beautifully colored.

There are many other plants that resemble grasses because of their grasslike blades. But the look-alikes are usually revealed when the plant flowers. It's then that these impostors typically sport petaled flowers instead of grasslike seed heads. See pages 48–52 for more on grass look-alikes and how to use them to advantage in your garden.

▼ About Nomenclature

In this book you will find both common and botanical names for the plants being discussed. Common names, while often lively and descriptive, may vary widely from region to region. A plant's botanical name, however, is the same throughout the world. To ensure that you are getting the grass that you want, always use the botanical name when buying plants. Do not be frightened of the botanical names. First,

remember that botanical names are nothing new. In the 1700s, when the present plant-naming system began, Latin was chosen because it was the international language of scholars and a dead language, which would not change. Don't worry if you're unsure how to pronounce Latin plant names; if you do your best, people will usually figure out what plant you are referring to.

The terms generally used to identify a particular plant are genus, species, variety, or cultivar. In print, genus and species names are typeset in italics (or in roman type if the text is in italics). The genus name always starts with a capital letter, and the species name is all lowercase. A variety of a species is a plant that differs from that species but not enough to be a species on its own. It is listed by its genus and species names, followed by a third Latin name (in italics), preceded by the abbreviation "var." Thus, bulbous oat grass is known as *Arrhenatherum elatius* var. *bulbosum.* A plant of botanical importance that has arisen in cultivation is called a cultivar (from *culti*vat*ed var*iety); its third name is capitalized, set in roman type, and enclosed in single quotes. Zebra grass, for example, is *Miscanthus sinensis* 'Zebrinus'.

▼ Grasses as Low-Maintenance Plants

Not only are grasses fascinating plants, they are also remarkably undemanding of the gardener. Ornamental grasses—whether annual or perennial—are virtually pest free, have the ability to withstand many environmental challenges, and as garden plants go, are almost foolproof.

Add these qualities to their inherent beauty, and it is obvious why ornamental grasses are gaining in popularity. They make it easy to have an eye-catching garden that requires relatively little care.

CHAPTER 1

Designing with Grasses

*a*mong the most versatile of plants, ornamental grasses can play many valuable roles in the garden. With a little design know-how, you can use them to create some of the most unusual and stunning gardens. • For instance, the same plant can serve as a subtle background to bright flowers in the summer and then command the landscape in winter, when its bold qualities emerge. By choosing appropriate ornamental grasses, you can add character to your garden. Use grasses to give a carefully planned garden a natural, even primitive look, as if you were letting the landscape return to its past. Or site specimen plants, to create a dramatic and deliberately artistic effect in the garden. • Easy to grow and care for, grasses allow you to enhance—even transform—any kind of environment.

In Beds or Masses

For years garden designers said that an entire garden of ornamental grasses would be dull, offering only boring repetition of linear grass blades. Then in 1980 the great British garden designer Russell Page proved how wrong this idea was. He landscaped the headquarters of PepsiCo, the soft-drink firm, in Purchase, New York, some 35 miles north of Manhattan. One of the theme gardens he planned consisted entirely of ornamental grasses. Since the unveiling of that garden, with its exciting visual rhythms, many more gardens have been designed around ornamental grasses.

Russell Page used bunches of maiden grass (*Miscanthus sinensis* 'Gracillimus'), allowing the plants to become a moving, sinuous chorus of green 6 to 8 feet wide and 7 feet high. In front of this screen he massed fountain grass (*Pennisetum alopecuroides*) and large swaths of the shorter but colorful variegated orchard grass (*Dactylis glomerata* 'Variegata') in free-form groups.

No matter how still the summer's day, at a certain time in the afternoon, when the air is the hottest but the ground begins to cool slightly, momentary breezes blow. The short blades of the fountain grasses sweep in one direction, while behind the taller maiden grasses dance in another direction. The effect is magical.

In late summer the grasses begin to bloom. It's astonishing to see all the grass blossoms waving rhythmically against a late-summer sky. In this season the feathery tan or buff blooms of fountain grass live up to their name, catching the light to suggest sparkling shafts of water. Beautiful at any time of the day, they are especially lovely early in the morning, when the rising sun illuminates every drop of dew that collects on the flowers' bristles.

Grasses can also look stunning in the evening. When statuesque members of the ornamental grass clan are underlit or illuminated with spotlights or garden lights, they become striking design elements.

Many of the larger grasses are effective when planted in masses. The *Miscanthus* species, pampas grass (*Cortaderia selloana*), prairie cordgrass (*Spartina pectinata*), reed grass (*Phragmites australis*)—as long as it is carefully contained—and a number of the larger bamboos are all outstanding when massed.

Pampas grass has become a kind of garden cliché, especially in the Southeast, where seemingly every roadside motel plants it on either side of the entrance sign. But when pampas grass plants are massed and combined with other grasses, especially fountain grasses, or planted with a backdrop of landscape bamboos or an evergreen hedge that sets off the silvery plumes of the pampas against the light of the setting sun, the result is pure delight.

Gardeners in warmer parts of the country, where the ground does not freeze deeply, can use khus-khus (*Vetiveria zizanioides*) in the garden. This Indian and Southeast Asian grass grows in tight vertical clumps about 3 feet wide and up to 8 feet high. The blades tend to bend over about 1 to 2 feet from the tip, making the plant look like a porcupine partially at rest. Khus-khus makes quite a garden statement when a number of plants are clumped together.

Smaller grasses also work well in masses. Japanese blood grass (*Imperata cylindrica* 'Red Baron') is all the more effective when you use a dozen plants rather than only one or two.

Natal grass, sometimes called champagne grass (*Rhynchelytrum repens*), is an invasive perennial in the South, but it is planted as an annual in the North.

Adding the weeping foliage of Japanese sedge (Carex morrowii) to the blue spruce and the rest of these plants makes the various leaf textures immediately apparent.

A mass planting of sedges in concert with other ornamental grasses results in a pleasing mix of colors, plant heights, leaf textures, and arching seed heads.

With this plant it's the blossoms that are glorious when many plants are grown together. The common name of champagne grass is perfectly appropriate because the light pink flower panicles stand at least 1 foot above the 2-foot balls of foliage. If planted on a hillside, they really look like the froth of champagne bubbling over the sides of a glass.

Gardeners in the Southwest can use Indian ricegrass *(Oryzopsis hymenoides)*, which bears its flowers in open panicles that become a gauzy screen of waving seed heads. This grass grows natively as far north as Manitoba in Canada, but it prefers warmer climates. It quickly dies if the soil is heavy and wet, especially during the cold months of winter.

If you are in doubt about the long-term uses of ornamental grasses in masses or clumps, experiment with a few of the annuals. For a small garden use a dozen or so plants of cloud grass *(Agrostis nebulosa)*, which give a cloudlike effect, as suggested by the common name. Or mass the silver blossoms of *Lamarckia aurea*. In a larger area, take advantage of the best ornamental corn, *Zea mays* var. *japonica*, an annual with variegated leaves that are longitudinally striped with green, white, and yellow, and sometimes highlighted with pink.

Grasses with Other Foliage

Grasses are versatile and mix easily with other plants. Luckily, there are a few ornamental grasses that do well in light shade, and some of the grass look-alikes respond to shade so well that they will grow in the company of ferns.

You could, for example, start with a centerpiece of sea oats *(Chasmanthium latifolium)* and surround it with variegated Japanese sedge grass *(Carex morrowii* 'Aureo-variegata'*)*. If you want to devote part of the garden to ferns, you might use Japanese painted fern *(Athyrium goeringianum* 'Pictum'*)* alongside *Carex pendula* and *C. conica* 'Variegata'. Add an underplanting of the beautiful yellow sedge *(Carex stricta* 'Bowles's Golden'*)* or golden wood millet *(Milium effusum* 'Aureum'*)* so that the light yellow stalks come up between the arching leaves of the various sedges. Wood millet is a cool-season grass that does not take well to steamy summers, so keep it out of hot sun and make sure the soil is always moist.

The giant fescue *(Festuca gigantea)*, which originally came from the open woods of Europe, is lovely when massed in woodland areas. Try planting this grass, with its arching leaves, to contrast with ferns, small hostas, or variegated ivies.

And don't overlook variegated silver grass *(Miscanthus sinensis* 'Variegatus')—it is eye-catching growing out of a clump of ivy. Variegated manna grass *(Glyceria maxima* 'Variegata'*)* especially likes moist or even wet soil, and grows beautifully in combination with some of the larger native ferns, such as the royal fern *(Osmunda regalis)* or ostrich fern *(Matteuccia pensylvanica)*. Most of these foliage combinations, however, do best in areas with cool summers and plenty of rainfall.

1 *The hosta planted in front of the stone wall makes a fine specimen plant, but too much dirt is visible and the composition lacks interest.*

2 *For contrast, add a golden-leaved grass, such as this Carex stricta 'Bowles's Golden'. Place a grass plant on each side of the hosta.*

Grasses with Flowers

At the Missouri Botanical Garden in St. Louis you can see a highly effective grouping of plants for a summer border. Next to a clump of goldenrod (*Solidago* spp.) and a number of obedient plants (*Physostegia virginiana*), there is a large fountain grass plant. In full bloom in late summer, its frothy panicles offer a marvelous contrast to the pinks and yellows of the other flowers. Here is proof again that grasses and flowers mix with ease.

Hedges are often used as a backdrop for flowers, but they are expensive and take time to grow; moreover, they are often out of scale in a small garden. Instead, you can use some of the large ornamental grasses to create the look of a hedge. Choose a grass species that will reach the approximate height you want when it matures, and plant a row of it. The

plants will form an attractive foliage backdrop for flowers, and will reach the desired size without requiring trimming and shearing. As a bonus, in most of the country you can also enjoy the splendid fall colors of ornamental grasses.

The beautiful flowing leaves of the golden-edged prairie cordgrass (*Spartina pectinata* 'Aureo-marginata') make a great hedge for an informal garden because their freewheeling growth avoids a static or controlled look.

In a small garden, a line of purple variegated moor grass (*Molinia caerulea* 'Variegata') presents mounds of leaves 1 to 3 feet high. For a 2-foot hedge use fountain grass; if you need a height of 3 to 5 feet, try the new pampas grass cultivar 'Pumila'.

A bed of perennials mixes flowering plants and ornamental grasses, including Calamagrostis, *in a bold composition. The tender* Echium wildpretii *at the right adds a touch of the exotic.*

Grasses with Flowers CONTINUED

Perennials to Grow with Grasses

A great many perennials can be grown along with ornamental grasses. Good choices include black-eyed Susans (Rudbeckia spp.); most of the taller goldenrods (Solidago spp.); the autumn-blooming asters, both tall and short varieties; hostas; daylilies; and Sedum 'Autumn Joy'.

Bulbs also make good companions for ornamental grasses. Try bright red Crocosmia or ornamental alliums, with their round heads of purple or white summer flowers.

For a tall hedge, plant one of the various miscanthus grasses. *Miscanthus sinensis* 'Morning Light' is a lovely plant with a light and airy feel to its graceful leaves; when planted close together, it makes a lovely hedge between 4 and 5 feet tall. *M. sinensis* 'Gracillimus' reaches 7 feet in height. For an even taller hedge, between 8 and 14 feet tall, rely on the imposing culms and blades of giant miscanthus *(M. floridulus)*.

A massing of giant reed *(Arundo donax)*, especially the variegated form, is a great foil for some of the

The copper-brown flowers of Pennisetum setaceum *'Cupreum' overlook a combination of annual plants, including* Coleus *'Pineapple Beauty' and Salvia 'Victoria'.*

shorter bush roses. The light green and white of its leaves blend to make an especially attractive background for the sturdy new Meidiland shrub roses, also known as landscape roses.

Brightly colored flowers become showstoppers when planted amid the quieter green tones of ornamental grasses. Imagine a bank of golden-edged prairie cordgrass *(Spartina pectinata* 'Aureo-marginata') with its attractive leaves tumbling gracefully in all directions. To create an effective contrast with the grass, add red, orange, and yellow daylilies *(Hemerocallis* spp.), as well as some wonderful goldenrod cultivars, such as *Solidago* 'Golden Fleece' and 'Crown of Rays'. To introduce a cool color note to the garden, include a steely blue dwarf conifer like *Juniperus squamata* 'Blue Star'. Such a garden will have color and movement throughout the growing season, and require little in the way of maintenance.

Anemones, including the charming Japanese varieties *(Anemone × hybrida)*, are also wonderful companions for grasses. When the late-summer flowers appear on top of the tall stems, their pinks and whites contrast charmingly with blue fescues or clumps of blue oat grass *(Helictotrichon sempervirens)*. Or combine the lovely sea oats *(Uniola paniculata)* with various members of the hellebore genus, especially Lenten roses *(Helleborus orientalis)*, which are available with pink, maroon, pale green, or creamy white flowers.

The thin blades of *Miscanthus sinensis* 'Morning Light' are lightly banded with white, and their shimmering effect offers a tremendous contrast to bright orange butterfly weed *(Asclepias tuberosa)* or pinkish purple prairie gay-feather *(Liatris* spp.).

One last combination to consider for your garden is to pair one of the oldest grass cultivars, *Miscanthus sinensis* 'Variegatus', with the daisylike flowers of

1 *Ornamental grasses (like the* Pennisetum *species shown) are very useful for softening color contrasts in the flower garden. This bed of annuals is full of intense, hot color.*

2 *Plant grasses among and around clumps of brightly colored flowers to tone down the contrast. Here, the grasses separate the bright colors and keep them from clashing.*

A Winning Combination
*Some of the most attractive mixes of flowers and grasses combine perennial grasses with quick-blooming annuals. An especially striking pairing is variegated bulbous oat grass (*Arrhenatherum elatius *var.* bulbosum *'Variegatum') and red pheasant's-eye (*Adonis aestivalis*). The blood-red of the pheasant's-eye blossoms goes well with the variegated grass, and both plants grow low to the ground.*

Rudbeckia species. The white-striped leaves of this variegated silver grass form a 4- to 6-foot mound that is a perfect foil for the deep gold of black-eyed Susans or red-and-gold gloriosa daisies.

The potential hue clashes of brightly colored flowers can be diffused by clever use of ornamental grasses. Imagine, for example, a block of pink anemones to the right and a planting of brilliant red bedding geraniums *(Pelargonium spp.)* to the left. If these plants were placed next to each other, the fight between the colors would be somewhat distracting. But if the flowers are divided by a curving line of the metallic blue foliage of sea Lyme grass *(Elymus arenarius)*, the bright colors will seem to meld into each other. The resulting arrangement is a pleasing color mixture rather than an eyesore.

Ornamental grasses can also be planted with bulbs. Hardy bulbs are the workhorses of perennial beds and borders. When properly treated (and if the foliage is allowed to ripen after flowering is over), the plants will continue to bloom year after year. But the problem with bulbs is the ripening foliage. When they are young and green, the leaves look fine, but when the leaf edges start to brown and curl at the tips, the plants are no longer attractive. Yet, nature demands that those leaves be left in place until they yellow and die, to help the bulb build up strength to bloom again next year.

Hostas and ferns make great companion plants for ripening bulbs in shady spots. But for bulbs that bloom in full sun, you can plant ornamental grasses close by to hide those browning bulb leaves behind their growing blades.

Grasses with Flowers CONTINUED

Try fescues to hide the ripening foliage of flowering onions *(Allium* spp.*)*, or *Stipa gigantea* to conceal the tawdry leaves of foxtail lilies *(Eremurus* spp.*)*. And while an entire hillside of daffodils in bloom is a delightful sign of returning spring, the profusion of floppy browning leaves that follow the bright yellow flowers can make the gardener think about moving them to a less prominent spot. If that hill is planted with fountain grasses, as the bulb leaves mature and turn brown the grasses will hide them.

Although grasses do not have blossoms like other flowering plants, you can create startling effects by combining ornamental grasses with some of the more unusual bulbs. The magic lily *(Lycoris squamigera)* is a good example. This bulb produces straplike leaves in spring that quickly die back, and all signs of a liv-

ing thing under the ground vanish for the summer. Then in late August to September, the flower stems arise, as if by magic, and grow to a height of up to 2 feet. These stems bear lovely pink trumpets, and with each succeeding year, more flowers appear. Try underplanting ornamental grasses with dozens of magic lilies. As summer comes to an end, a host of lilies will appear to delight you and anyone who visits. Gardeners in USDA zone 7 and south can also grow the lovely red spider lily *(L. sanguinea)*, which is a close relative.

1 *A pleasant perennial bed with blooming lycoris* (L. squamigera) *appears to be divided by the lines of visible dirt. This dirt detracts from the other plants.*

2 *Add some small grasses to fill the empty spaces and introduce different textures. Arrange the grasses while they are still in their pots to make sure you like the composition.*

3 *The new grasses provide both contrasting texture and a pleasing background to the pink flowers of the lycoris and the sedum coming into bloom on the right.*

Grasses with Shrubs

As described on pages 15–16, ornamental grasses are terrific for making a quick-growing hedge. But because of the stature attained by some of the large species and cultivars—not to mention the stately aspect of many bamboos—grasses also look great when combined with shrubs.

For example, the foliage of winged-bark euonymus *(Euonymus alata)* turns a brilliant red in the fall and becomes a startling accent when planted with any of the larger *Miscanthus* species. A line of evergreen rhododendrons can easily be lightened up with the addition of short grasses. Blue fescues *(Festuca ovina* var. *glauca)* can hide the leafless lower stems of a row of old boxwoods *(Buxus sempervirens)*. And nothing beats a few plants of sea oats set in front of the magnificent American native shrub, the oakleaf hydrangea *(H. quercifolia)*.

Other good shrubs to plant with ornamental grasses include garland flower *(Daphne cneorum)*, sweet box *(Sarcococca hookerana)*, heaths and heathers, dwarf junipers, brooms *(Cytisus* spp.)*, and species of shrub roses.

Shrubs and ornamental grasses can be combined to great effect in the garden. Here, fountain grass (Pennisetum) *mixes with dwarf conifers, colorful impatiens, and coleus.*

Annual Grasses

*T*here are about 20 annual grasses to be found in seed catalogues today. Most of these grasses are true annuals, blooming and setting seed over the course of one summer. A few are tropical perennials that will persist year after year in frost-free climates, but because they bloom the first year from seed they are considered to be annuals by most gardeners. These annual grasses are grown not for their foliage—which is usually weedy—but for their flowers and seed heads, which are always spectacular.

Some annuals, like the cloud grasses *(Agrostis* spp.*)* or goldentop *(Lamarckia aurea)*, make elegant border edgings. Others are best when massed between other perennials. Goldentop is lovely in small gardens, as are most of the brome grasses *(Bromus* spp.*)*. For soft texture in a small space, try a small new cultivar of hare's-tail grass *(Lagurus ovatus* 'Nana'*)*, with its fuzzy little cottontail blossoms. The larger foxtail millet *(Setaria italica)*, black sorghum *(Sorghum bicolor* var. *technicus)*, and variegated corn are best in a bigger garden setting.

Another attractive annual grass is animated oats *(Avena sterilis)*, a larger version of wild oats *(A. fatua)*. The plant got the name "animated oats" because the awns (bristlelike appendages that stick out from its seeds) begin to move whenever the humidity changes.

The addition of a clump or two of a colorful or interesting annual grass can bring a sense of counterpoint to a bed or border of perennial flowers.

Annual grasses can fill areas between perennial plants, and they reliably bloom a few months after sowing. The delightful flower heads of hare's-tail grass (Lagurus ovatus) *resemble their namesakes. Long after the garden has gone to bed they are valuable as dried flowers.*

Grasses in Specialty Gardens

Creating a garden with a particular theme can conjure up a sense of place, set a mood, or achieve a specific goal. Ornamental grasses can take on a whole new personality when used in specialty gardens combined with other carefully chosen plants. Grasses are particularly effective in Japanese gardens, rock gardens, and cutting gardens.

▼ Japanese Gardens

Japanese gardens depend on foliage and plant form, with less emphasis on flowers, so they are ideal for ornamental grasses.

Within a Japanese garden design, ornamental grasses are especially effective when planted among carefully placed rocks. Good choices include members of the genus *Miscanthus* (they are originally from East Asia); some of the smaller grasses with spiky foliage, such as fescue cultivars; and Japanese blood grass, which turns brilliant red in the fall. Bamboos, the backbone of many gardens in Japan, strike a beautiful, authentic note in theme gardens grown in this country. To complete the look, cover any bare soil in the garden with a mulch of gravel or small pebbles.

▼ Rock Gardens

Rock gardens usually feature small alpine plants that want perfect drainage and are found in nature growing at high elevations in rock outcrops or directly in fields of crushed stone. Many of the smaller ornamental grasses have fibrous roots that adapt to rock garden sites. Just as in Japanese gardens, the texture and the color of the grass leaves augment the beauty of the stones.

A Japanese-style garden of ferns is enhanced by the use of bamboo. The wood posts are not only decorative but also act as barriers to the bamboo's possible advances.

Grasses that work well in rock gardens include Japanese blood grass, hare's-tail grass, blue oat grass, blue grama *(Bouteloua gracilis)*, striped orchard grass *(Dactylis glomerata* 'Variegata'), most of the fescues, and the annual and perennial fountain grasses.

▼ Cutting Gardens

Cutting gardens are planted to produce flowers for home decoration, table centerpieces, and dried bouquets to brighten up the winter months. Many of the perennial ornamental grasses have a place in this type of garden, not only for their flowers, but also for their foliage, which can take the place of the fern fronds typically included in arrangements. Annual grasses, too, are good for cutting and drying. When the marvelous flowers and seed heads are cut, you can sow a second crop to produce more material for cutting and drying later in the season.

Grasses as Transitions

Ornamental grasses have many landscape uses. They can be planted to buffer brightly colored flowers, as described earlier, or they can be used as living walls to separate various "rooms" in the garden. You can also plant a line of larger grasses or even bamboo as a screen to hide an undesirable view or create privacy. Since these plants are very long-lived, a 3-foot gap could be left for a charming gate.

Ornamental grasses can also provide a transition between different parts of the landscape, such as woodland and meadow, or they can help blend a water garden into its surroundings.

The feeling of a woodland or wild garden is often at odds with the more controlled look of the formal garden bed or border. Going directly from neatly mowed grass or well-kept pathways into a wooded area gives the landscape an artificial feeling. But adding a line of grasses, such as *Festuca gigantea*, or one of the sedges, such as *Carex conica* 'Variegata' or *C. morrowii* 'Variegata', softens that distinct edge and makes the landscape look more realistic.

A similar effect can be achieved with grasses planted between a garden and a meadow. The shift from low-lying cultivated ground to meadow grasses and wildflowers that are often up to 5 or 6 feet tall will appear far more natural if ornamental grasses are used to bridge the gap.

Going directly from cultivated ground to large areas of water is rarely successful in a garden without some kind of demarcation between the two environments. Small pools can be edged with bricks or stonework, but large ponds or small lakes benefit greatly from having plants along their borders. Ornamental grasses, with their free-flowing form, can suggest the movement of water, setting the stage for the pond.

Except for grass species unique to deserts or open meadows, most of the larger ornamental grasses and grass look-alikes—such as sweet flag (*Acorus* spp.), horsetail (*Equisetum hyemale*), cattails (*Typha* spp.), sedges, and rushes—thrive with wet or moist feet. The reflection in the water turns one plant into two, creating a beautiful mirror image of the garden.

*The soft waving plumes
of autumn-blooming*
Miscanthus sinensis *cultivars
provide a low-maintenance
transition to the woods in
the rear.*

Architectural Uses

The tall marble pillars of a very formal garden are relieved by the waving, metallic blue blades of blue wild rye (Elymus glaucus). *Used alone or in masses, this grass adapts to meadows and dry hillsides and is also excellent in a rock garden.*

Wolfgang Oehme, James van Sweden, and their Washington, D.C.–based firm of landscape architects pioneered the use of ornamental grasses in public places, including sites that seemed inhospitable to plants. Through their influence, ornamental grasses are increasingly replacing typical displays of colorful bedding plants in parks and other public places.

Ornamental grasses are well suited to city life. Many have fibrous roots that run deep into the soil. As a result, once they have adapted to their place in the earth, it takes a lot more than heat, lack of water, and city fumes to do them in.

Today as you drive through many American cities, you will find installations of the larger ornamental grasses (and occasionally bamboos) in front of public buildings, hospitals, and office complexes. And if you drive by many of these public buildings at night, you will see that the drama of the grasses by day is doubled at night when they are illuminated by spotlights or other garden lights.

▼ Lighting Grass Gardens at Night

Small areas of your garden, especially where ornamental grasses are planted, can be illuminated by what is called mood lighting. This lighting is adequately handled by a 12-volt system. If you need to light a larger area or if you wish for large-scale lighting with pronounced dramatic effects, you will probably need a 120-volt system. Or you might use both types of lighting in different parts of the garden. Gentler parts of the garden can be wired with 12-volt lights while featured plantings—perhaps a combination of shrubs and large ornamental grasses (such as giant reed, *Arundo donax*)—can be lit with a 120-volt outdoor fluorescent lamp.

Architectural Uses CONTINUED

Before you select lighting it's important to know that there are various levels of light intensity. Recognizing these differences will enable you to evaluate a light manufacturer's claims.

Light is measured in levels of brightness called foot-candles. A foot-candle is the amount of light cast on a white surface by one candle, 1 foot away, in an otherwise dark room.

The lowest light is dim light. The best example of dim light is the light cast by a full moon. This is about a tenth of a foot-candle.

Medium-bright light varies between ½ and 7 or 8 foot-candles. Most individual low-voltage garden fixtures produce 1 foot-candle of light, while fixtures in the 120-volt range can go up to 5 foot-candles.

Bright light is equal to 8 foot-candles or more. A comfortable light for reading is 50 foot-candles, and the light level in most stores and offices is more than 100 foot-candles. While some trees or areas in an evening garden could be illuminated to a brightness of 20 foot-candles, most areas would be best at 5 or below.

There are a number of techniques for lighting plants, as described below and on the next page.

▼ **Downlighting or Area Lighting**

If lamps are placed high up in trees so that the light points down toward the ground, they cast a wide path of light. This lighting method easily illuminates your lawn or garden and opens up these areas for evening entertainment while also providing nighttime security. When lights are positioned closer to the ground, they can highlight flower beds, pathways, or steps.

A row of pampas grass (Cortaderia selloana) *forms a low-maintenance hedge that provides not only tall clumps of airy blades but also, in late summer, a bonus of tall plumelike flower heads that persist for weeks.*

Plant a row or large clump of tall grasses, such as the variegated silver grass (Miscanthus sinensis *'Variegatus'*) *shown here, to provide privacy or screen off an undesirable view.*

▼ Accent Lighting

Lights are often used to train a brighter beam on focal points in the garden, including favorite specimen grasses, small trees, or garden sculpture. Accent lighting is easy to overdo, turning your garden into a light show. When there are too many spotlights, your attention is pulled from light to light instead of drifting slowly over the scene. Use caution when planning your spotlighting design.

▼ Silhouetting

This beautiful effect is achieved by placing lights below sight level, in front of a wall or other vertical surface, so that the wall is washed with soft light. Ornamental grasses or bamboos in front of that wall will create the same effect as mountains against a twilit sky.

▼ Shadowing

This method is much like silhouetting, except the light is placed in front of an object so that its shadow will fall on the wall or screen behind it. Shadowing can create a subtly evocative scene, especially when soft winds move the leaves and branches of plants like bamboos or grasses.

▼ Pool and Fountain Lighting

Special underwater lights are available for creating very dramatic effects in small ornamental pools. A pot of horsetails, lit from below with a halogen light, will leave visitors stunned by the beauty of the scene.

Alternatives to Lawns

While you may not want to turn your front lawn into a wilderness, you can remove the traditional creeping grasses from at least part of your lawn and trade them in for some ornamental grasses. These ornamental grasses will look fantastic and free you considerably from the maintenance chores needed for a perfectly manicured lawn.

You can use grasses to create a feeling of sunny meadows of waving plants. Some good possibilities are eulalia grasses *(Miscanthus* spp.*)*, feather reed grass *(Calamagrostis acutiflora* var. *stricta)*, the always spectacular maiden grass *(Miscanthus sinensis* 'Gracillimus')*, and two fountain grasses, *Pennisetum alopecuroides* and *P. orientale.*

Many gardeners have traded in a part of the lawn and replaced it with ground covers, especially ivy *(Hedera* spp.*)* and *Pachysandra.* An alternative, in areas of USDA zone 6 and warmer, is the marvelous pygmy bamboo *(Arundinaria pygmaea).* Pygmy bamboo makes an aggressive and effective ground cover, and if it gets out of hand you can just cut it back with a lawn mower.

The concept of the island bed was originally popularized by Alan Bloom, a highly knowledgeable English gardener and nurseryman with a marvelous imagination. He wrote about carving oval beds out of the lawn and filling them with assorted perennials to brighten up a dull expanse of green and bring more variety into the garden. You can create an island bed in the middle of your lawn and plant it with ornamental grasses to make the lawn more interesting and decrease the amount of grass you have to mow (see the sidebar on page 27).

An island of bed grasses and low-maintenance perennials combines Miscanthus sinensis *(left),* M. sinensis *var.* purpurescens, *and* Sedum 'Autumn Joy', *which blooms in late summer and fall.*

Low-growing grasses can make good ground covers when planted in masses, as long as you put them where they will not be trampled upon. In this garden, low grasses edge the path and combine with shrubs and other perennials to weave a tapestry of foliage textures.

Sedges can be planted in masses as a ground cover to substitute for lawn in an area not subject to foot traffic. This one is Carex comans 'Frosty Curls'.

Less Lawn to Mow

If you are tired of cutting all that lawn, try clearing a large circle or oval of garden toward the center of the yard and planting it with a collection of ornamental grasses. The high point of this island bed could be one mature Ravenna grass plant (Erianthus ravennae), a few of the larger eulalia grasses, or in warmer parts of the country, one of the new pampas grass cultivars. Then surround that planting with a ring of fountain grasses and finish off the edges with a line of dwarf fescues. You still have the lawn, but all you need to maintain the ornamental grasses are sharpened shears to cut back last year's growth at the end of February or early in March.

Grasses as Living Sculpture

For a smaller garden, try planting horsetails (Equisetum spp.). These evergreen perennial grasses are truly sculptural, and if properly displayed, they look as though they were made by an Italian artist instead of nature. Or use horsetails as a short-term houseplant in a very simple container; plant them in a water garden; or mass them together in front of a plain or textured wall. They make ideal accent plants for a troublesome wet spot.

For little gardens, there are small grasses that still pack an architectural punch. Here, a dwarf variety of pampas grass (Cortaderia selloana) has a commanding presence when used by itself in the middle of a lawn.

*F*ew perennial plants are as impressive as a clump of ornamental grasses, especially when you consider that they start anew each spring. Clumps of ornamental grasses—even common grasses—can be as striking as a piece of outdoor sculpture.

As described earlier, pampas grass has become something of a cliché throughout the South because it's overused. But when a specimen of pampas grass is perfectly sited and surrounded by enough open space, it becomes an eye-catching living construction.

Many of the large grasses have a monumental quality that is really noticeable when they are isolated in the landscape or are viewed against a hill. These grasses are stunning when planted in front of a wall (especially a textured surface).

The giant reed *(Arundo donax)* sports large canes and reaches an average height of 9 feet; a big clump of these grasses in an island bed becomes an arresting focal point in the landscape. Or, instead of giant reed, try a planting of Ravenna grass *(Erianthus ravennae)*, whose 12-foot shafts topped with fluffy flower plumes will wave in the wind.

At night the drama can be doubled by backlighting or spotlighting these grasses with the regular or low-voltage lights described on page 24.

For a very special effect, grow a clump of giant miscanthus *(Miscanthus floridulus)*. Even in USDA zone 5, this grass will reach a height of 8 to 14 feet by the end of July.

Design Qualities of Grasses

Grasses can exhibit two types of growth habits. Running grasses, also known as creeping grasses, spread by creeping underground stems. The other type, clumping grasses, grows in tufts and forms clumps or bunches. Running grasses are often invasive. Most running grasses have little ornamental quality, and their use is limited to lawns except for a few, such as buffalo grass *(Buchloe dactyloides)*.

When choosing grasses to star in a design, most gardeners prefer the clumping grasses because they stay in one place, often becoming larger with each year of growth. Clumping grasses come in a surprising number of forms, textures, color, and heights that remain constant within each species. These qualities are described and illustrated on the following pages.

▼ Form

Ornamental grasses are available in dozens of different shapes and sizes. The following five forms exemplify the various types of growth:

Tufted grasses have upright, usually narrow foliage arising from a clump. They are best represented by the fescues *(Festuca spp.)*.

Mounded species form thick, arching clumps of leaves that are often so dense they are striking even when not in flower. One of the best mound-forming grasses is the new cultivar *Pennisetum alopecuroides* 'Moudry'.

Upright plants have foliage that is uniformly vertical, a growth form especially noticeable in khus-khus *(Vetiveria zizanioides)*, cattail *(Typha spp.)*, and especially many of the *Molinia caerulea* cultivars like 'Windspiel' and 'Skyracer'.

The ornamental grass beds in the garden at PepsiCo headquarters in Purchase, New York, display a wide selection of grasses, including blue fescues, fountain grasses, and clumps of maiden grass in the distance.

Design Qualities of Grasses CONTINUED

Upright divergent grasses look like hedgehogs or porcupines: the leaves grow up and out in straight lines. Blue oat grass *(Helictotrichon sempervirens)* and the larger fescues are good examples of this form.

Arching grasses grow up from the ground and then arch and bend over. Purple moor grass *(Molinia caerulea)* and the fountain grasses *(Pennisetum* spp.*)* are good examples of this growth form.

The plumes and blades of the common miscanthus (M. sinensis) are graceful in the wind.

Horsetails (Equisetum hyemale) are not grasses but much more primitive plants, with a stiff, upright stance.

Blue oat grass (Helictotrichon sempervirens) makes small upright, then spreading, fountains of steely blue.

For a larger fountain effect, try the graceful maiden grass (Miscanthus sinensis 'Gracillimus').

Golden variegated hakonechloa (Hakonechloa macra 'Aureola') makes soft mounds of variegated foliage.

California fescue (Festuca californica 'Serpentine Blue') is a warm-climate grass with tufted form.

▼ Texture

In terms of plants, texture refers to the physical properties of the leaves and flowers. A blade of grass may be smooth with a thin midrib that may be hardly noticeable, or it may have a sandpaper-like surface and a prominent midrib. The culm can be thin like wire or as thick as a closet rod to hang clothes upon.

Some grasses have dozens of thin, spikelike leaves. Others, like the *Miscanthus* species, have leaves that run up the culm and, by the time they reach the top, are overlapped many times. The leaves have a sheen that reflects light, giving the plant an almost luminous presence in the landscape.

In many of the grasses, when the blades are a blue color they are called blooms. The blue color is the result of a fine, powdery surface that does not reflect light. On the other hand, some grasses—notably the sedges *(Carex* spp.)—have leaves with a highly polished surface. All of these differences in leaf structure change the way light falls upon the plants, and therefore how they look in the garden. The open and airy aspect of the flowers and seed heads adds yet another dimension to the total texture of a plant.

▼ Color

You may not think of ornamental grasses as colorful plants, so you might be surprised by their color range (see pages 32–33). In addition to the various shades of greens, there are also blues, reds, oranges, tans, and in summer, variegated patterns in some cultivars. With the coming of winter many of the ornamental grasses change to various shades of gold, beige, and brown. When designing your garden of grasses, you could treat each plant as part of a richly colored piece of three-dimensional fabric.

▼ Height

Grasses come in a remarkable variety of heights, ranging from a few inches for the small fescues to the 14 feet of giant miscanthus *(M. floridulus)*. To get a perspective of their scale in the garden, consider the larger grasses the same size as large shrubs or small trees.

▼ Garden Compositions

When working with grasses, consider all of the plant qualities discussed on pages 29–34. By alternating and manipulating these various design qualities—form, color, leaf and flower textures, and height—you can create a harmonious, pleasing design in the garden. While much of design is determined by the personal taste of the gardener, there are a few guidelines that can make your choices easier and more successful.

For example, subtle differences of texture and color are most visible in the soft light of shady gardens, because they are likely to go unnoticed in the glare of the hot summer sun. Bolder plants, however, such as blue fescues, sea Lyme grass, and Japanese blood grass, look all the more vivid in the strong light of open, sunny locations.

Large grasses, like *Miscanthus* species or giant reed *(Arundo donax)*, create divisions in the landscape. Due to their size, they are often most effective when used as a background for other grasses and flowering plants. Or you can treat them as specimens (focal points) and plant them by themselves in the yard.

On the other hand, when designing with smaller grasses in the bed or border, try to place them so that various shapes overlap each other rather than allowing each plant to stand by itself.

To achieve various heights in the garden, ornamental grasses are often easier to use than perennials. Here, a short sedge (Carex spp.) and a somewhat taller switchgrass (Panicum virgatum) are backed by dwarf pampas grass (Cortaderia selloana 'Pumila'), giving a terraced effect.

Some grasses are especially effective when they are massed together. Always work with odd numbers of plants unless regimentation is part of your garden theme. For example, three or five variegated moor grass plants *(Molinia caerulea* 'Variegata'*)* are stunning when surrounded by other flowering plants.

Or you could create a sinuous planting as festive as Carnival in Rio by grouping an assortment of fescues in straight or curving lines along a sidewalk.

Whatever advice you read or hear, always remember it's your garden and its look should please you. The mistakes of one year may look like triumphs to you another year.

Leaf Color and Variegation

TROUBLESHOOTING TIP

If you live in a northern climate where zebra grass (Miscanthus sinensis 'Zebrinus') will not survive, try planting the closely related porcupine grass (M. sinensis 'Strictus'). One of the newer variegated plants available at nurseries, porcupine grass is hardier than zebra grass (it survives in zone 4), and its form is also different. Zebra grass has gracefully arching leaves, while porcupine grass has ½-inch-wide, banded blades that stick out from the culms at a 45° angle. The plants reach 6 feet high and are especially beautiful in a waterside planting.

Plant variegation for ornamental grasses is defined as yellow, white, or cream-colored markings on leaves that are otherwise green. The light patches, streaks, stripes, spots, or splashes are caused by an absence of chlorophyll. Variegation can be due to a number of disease reactions (including a virus infection), but in many cases it can be traced to a hereditary defect that does not hurt the plant. Most variegated plants are not as strong as their pure green relatives and need more tempered growing conditions. A plant normally conditioned to full sun, for instance, will often prefer a bit of shade in its variegated form. Some of the variegations are so entrenched in the genetic pattern of the plants that seedlings will continue to display the defect. Usually, however, variegated plants must be reproduced by vegetative means.

Grasses display a number of different variegation patterns. Many beautiful plants have appeared over the years and more are still being discovered by plant explorers or nursery owners.

Horticulturists have always delighted in variegated plants (much to the dismay of purists), and when used properly, these grasses lend a unique pattern and texture to the garden.

Probably the first variegated grass on the market was the white-striped variety of giant reed *(Arundo donax* var. *variegata)*, which appeared in Europe in 1863. The creamy white variegations run longitudinally along the blades in varying widths. Unfortunately, the reed grass itself is only marginally hardy in USDA zone 6, or it would be far more popular in American gardens.

Two of the best variegated grasses were developed in English nurseries during the last century. In 1877 zebra grass *(Miscanthus sinensis* 'Zebrinus'), called tiger grass in England, became available. This plant's variegation is a soft yellow, appearing as horizontal dabs that march up each leaf. Somehow the variegation is cued to temperature—it does not appear until mid-July.

The second is variegated silver grass *(Miscanthus sinensis* 'Variegatus'), which has stems tinted with pink and long blades striped longitudinally with white. This cultivar was first marketed in 1896.

A somewhat more recent introduction is purple variegated moor grass *(Molinia caerulea* 'Variegata'). This plant is believed to have originated in Germany sometime before World War II. (Until World War II

For vibrant color, one of the best grasses is Japanese blood grass (Imperata cylindrica *var.* rubra). *It's excellent in front stone walls or massed to contrast with green or blue foliage.*

The striped variegations of zebra grass (Miscanthus sinensis *'Zebrinus') are unusual in the world of ornamental grasses. The plants are beautiful when used as specimen plants or massed in a large border.*

The blossoms of Korean feather reed grass (Calamagrostis arundinacea *'Karl Foerster') give off an autumnal bronze glow.*

Germany was probably the most important country for the introduction of new grass cultivars.) The foliage of variegated moor grass forms a neat, compact mound that is useful in either flower beds or rock gardens. It is variegated with thin horizontal stripes of white. But the flowers and flower stems are the most unusual part of this plant. They, too, are variegated, as though an elf with a tiny paintbrush had touched them with dabs of white.

Zebra grass, variegated silver grass, and variegated moor grass were the most popular of the variegated line until the recent introduction of *Miscanthus sinensis* 'Morning Light', a superb plant found in Japan in 1976 by well-respected plant hunters John Creech and Skip March.

Other outstanding variegated grasses include striped orchard grass *(Dactylis glomerata* 'Variegata'*)*, which appeared on the market in 1935. This cultivar has soft leaves of grayish green, and each blade is edged with creamy white.

Leaf Color and Variegation CONTINUED

Variegated bulbous oat grass *(Arrhenatherum elatius* var. *bulbosum* 'Variegatum*)* came along sometime after 1953. The common name comes from the plants' bulblike bottoms; they are really swollen stem nodes, but they look like bulbs. The variegations are thin white stripes on medium green leaves. This cool-season grass gives its best performance in spring and fall.

No discussion of variegation would be complete without mentioning golden variegated hakone grass *(Hakonechloa macra* 'Aureola*)*. The plant, which first appeared in Japan in 1930, is a distinct brilliant yellow that is streaked with green. In the fall, each blade is lightly touched with varying shades of pink. As with most variegated plants, too much sun tends to burn the leaves. For the best display, plant this grass in high, open shade.

▼ Grasslike Plants with Variegations

Some of the grass look-alikes have variegated forms that are very useful in the garden. At the top of the line are probably the white and yellow stripings found in various cultivars of *Carex morrowii*, including 'Variegata', in which the edges of each leaf are highlighted with silver, and 'Goldband', where the color is distinctly yellow. The graceful leaves of another sedge, *C. conica* 'Variegata', are edged with a very thin strip of silvery white.

An unusual grasslike plant is the striped bulrush *(Schoenplectus tabernaemontana* 'Zebrinus*)*. Often called the porcupine plant, this spikelike plant has horizontal stripes of white that are spaced evenly up (or down) each stem. Striped bulrush grows best in shallow water and does quite well in pots.

The variegated grasslike leaves of lilyturf (Liriope muscari 'Variegata) *bring a bright sparkle to a shady area, especially near a small pond or pool. In warmer areas the leaves persist through the winter. The spikes of small blue flowers that emerge in summer are a bonus.*

Flowers of Grasses

Because grasses depend only on wind for pollination, they have no need for extensive and magnificent floral displays with garish petals and sweet nectars to attract bees, ants, beetles, and birds to complete the job of pollination. The grasses simply let their pollen float into the air, and it is carried from flower to flower by the wind.

The flower parts of grasses are essentially the same as those of other plants, but some of the features have become modified. The petals have all but disappeared, and the other parts of the flowers are so small that you need a magnifying glass to see them clearly.

Usually both male and female parts are found within the same blossom. The ovary is topped with plumed stigmas specially designed by nature to pick other pollen grains right out of the air. Below the stigmas are large stamens, with anthers at the end that produce pollen. The stamens can easily cast pollen grains to the breeze.

Because of the dependence on wind pollination, many of the grasses' ripening seed heads are open to the air (as opposed to being enclosed in a fruit or capsule). The seed heads are light and often fluffy. They are beautiful in the garden when fresh, and many are stunning when dried, making exceptionally attractive additions to dried arrangements.

To make sure that grasses produce enough seeds for the continuation of each species, every plant bears many individual flowers that are gathered together in clusters. These clusters (or inflorescences) are made up of subdivisions called spikelets. The spikelets are arranged in variations of three different forms: terminal spikes, as found in the flowers of the magnificent

The flowers of two grasses, fountain grass (Pennisetum alopecuroides) *and purple maiden grass* (Miscanthus sinensis *var.* purpurescens), *take on beautiful colors in the fall, and the magnificent seed heads will persist through the winter.*

Flowers of Grasses CONTINUED

Whatever the species or variety, Miscanthus *blossoms are glorious when opening in late summer or early fall, still beautiful when snow falls, and great as dried flowers.*

*The delicate, airy blossoms of frost grass (*Spodiopogon sibiricus*) are among the most beautiful of all the grasses. It's at its best in cooler areas with moist, fertile soil.*

*The soft-textured blossoms of all the fountain grasses (*Pennisetum *spp.) are especially beautiful when planted so that the rays of the rising or setting sun can reflect on the bristles.*

eulalia grasses *(Miscanthus* spp.*)*; panicles, as evidenced by flowers of natal grass *(Rhynchelytrum repens)*; and racemes, a form that makes the beautiful seed heads of grasses like the bromes *(Bromus* spp.*)*.

Many grasses flower with such precise timing that you could set a watch by their blooming habits. The flowers of quaking grasses open at about 6:00 A.M. and the brome flowers open at 2:00 P.M. The process begins when the flower parts open, allowing the anthers to spread and shake their pollen into the wind while the feathery stigmas of another flower are ready to receive the pollen. Grasses rarely self-fertilize; they are usually sterile to their own pollen.

The seeds of grasses assume many sizes and shapes, all of which are readily adapted to dispersal by the wind, by animals, or by humans. Many of the brome grasses have seeds with barbed tips that easily cling to animals' hairs or people's clothes and may actually drive their pointed tips directly into an animal's skin. Other seeds exhibit long and attractive plumes that let them float through the air just like dandelion or milkweed fluff. People have often been active agents in the spread of grasses. For example, African grasses (such as Bermuda grass and molasses grass) were used for bedding in slave ships and soon began to grow at all ports-of-call.

The flowers and eventual seed heads of zebra grass (Miscanthus sinensis 'Zebrinus'), seen here in late autumn, have a very long season of bloom. Unless torn apart by fierce winds, they will often persist until late winter.

Three typical types of flowers found on ornamental grasses are, left to right, a terminal spike, as is found on hare's-tail grass (Lagurus ovatus); a raceme, exemplified by manna grass (Glyceria spp.); and a panicle, like the flowers of orchard grass (Dactylis spp.).

Grasses Through the Seasons

Cool-Season Grasses

Cool-season grasses don't thrive in heat and seem to sulk in areas where summers are hot and humid. You may wish to avoid planting these grasses if you live in such a climate. Cool-season grasses include many of the hair grasses (Deschampsia spp.), the melic grasses (Melica spp.), most of the sedges and rushes, and the stipas, including Stipa gigantea.

When the weather gets hot, the following grasses actually turn brown: variegated velvet grass (Holcus lanatus var. variegatus), silky-spike melic (Melica ciliata), golden wood millet (Milium effusum 'Aureum'), and bottlebrush grass (Hystrix patula).

In this Northwest garden, bright green leaves of young Hakonechloa macra 'Aureola' emerge in spring at the same time as hellebores and anemones bloom.

Most flowering perennials have short seasons when their blossoms are a garden delight. Then the flowers fade until the next year. Such is not the case with most ornamental grasses. Some are evergreen, and after suffering some of winter's cold, they quickly produce new leaves. Others flower in the spring, and still others bloom in summer. Most of the late-summer bloomers hold their flowers until well into winter, accompanied by colorful changes in leaf color with the first frosts.

The sedges and rushes are mostly spring-blooming plants. While their flowers are interesting but rarely spectacular, their fresh spring foliage positively glows in the garden. While many grasses and grass look-alikes bloom later in the year, in the spring you can look for the blossoms of tufted hair grass *(Deschampsia caespitosa)*, whose airy panicles persist well into summer. The tall, light yellow panicles of feather reed grass *(Calamagrostis acutiflora* var. *stricta)* are also visible in spring and last until late in the year. In late May the flower spikes of large blue hair grass *(Koeleria glauca)* burst forth, as do the white, showy

The wonderful colors of a summer garden are highlighted by the airy fountains of two varieties of Miscanthus, *which make a perfect backdrop.*

TROUBLESHOOTING TIP

When the lower portion of the blades of giant miscanthus (Miscanthus floridulus) *begin to brown with summer's heat, simply remove them to a height of about 6 feet. It won't hurt the plant and you will be left with dozens of straight bamboo-like stems topped with arching fountains of green. This is a dramatic sight to see by day or by night.*

spikelike panicles of the silky-spike melic grass *(Melica ciliata)*, which often last until July. In late spring 2-foot-high one-sided panicles appear on top of blue oat grass *(Helictotrichon sempervirens)*.

All of these grasses are known as cool-season grasses and are at their best in spring because they prefer daytime temperatures around 65°F.

Summer is the time for the warm-season grasses to gear up for growth and bloom. Fountain grasses *(Pennisetum spp.)* have a spurt of growth in summer and then flower, with the aging seed heads lasting well into fall (in warm climates they begin flowering in spring). Japanese blood grass *(Imperata cylindrica* 'Red Baron'*)* begins to color in summer. The molinias also bloom, holding their blossoms over fresh, arching foliage. Sea oats *(Uniola paniculata)* spring forth with green oatlike blossoms that eventually turn to brown as the summer advances. The distinctive yellow bands now appear on the leaves of porcupine and zebra grasses. All the annual grasses planted in spring also burst into bloom in summer.

Autumn is probably the most spectacular time for ornamental grasses. At this time of year most of the

Grasses Through the Seasons CONTINUED

TIMESAVING TIP

The best time to move grasses is in the winter or early spring, after you have removed as much of the foliage as possible. The traditional way to remove the foliage is to light a small bonfire and burn off the old leaves. It won't hurt the grasses, but be careful to burn only in wet weather and get a permit when one is required.

Most ornamental grasses achieve their greatest impact in fall. Here, Calamagrostis acutiflora *var.* stricta, *far left, and* Schizachyrium scoparium *are divided by* Sedum *'Autumn Joy' and* Amsonia tabernaemontana *var.* salicifolia.

large species, including eulalias and pampas grasses, bloom. The eulalia blossoms continue to bend and shift in the fall breezes until they are touched by the first snows of early winter. There are also still blossoms left over from the summer-blooming fountain grasses, only now the leaves turn from green to light tan. With the shortening days, the soft blades of many grasses begin to stiffen, and if you missed the seasonal changes in color, you will surely note the changes in sound, as the soft rustlings become slightly harsher.

Gardeners who live where the growing season is short, where winter arrives about Thanksgiving and often stays until late April, quickly develop a special love for grasses in the winter.

When the arching plumes of *Miscanthus* are lightly brushed with that first snowfall, gardeners may feel as if they were standing in an exquisite garden in Tokyo instead of in a backyard in the Midwest. In fact, all of the *Miscanthus* grasses persist for a long time, even when buffeted by stiff winter winds. Prairie cordgrass *(Spartina pectinata)* will also endure climatic indignities for weeks before the blades begin to look tattered and torn.

In winter, when the taller grasses and bamboos are brushed with snow, the garden is still beautiful and begins to look like a Japanese drawing. •

TIMESAVING TIP

If you haven't removed the bottom leaves on your miscanthus (Miscanthus floridulus) *by the time winter approaches, the winds of late December will do it for you, revealing the stout culms that are tinged with reds and orange. The plants will stand like sentinels against the winter skyline.*

In the winter, fountain grass and purple moor grass both bring to mind the frozen waters of a garden sprinkler that you forgot to turn off. Fountain grass is a lovely shade of brown, and purple moor grass is truly golden.

Feather reed grass *(Calamagrostis acutiflora* var. *stricta)* has thinner blades than those of most other grasses. They stand straight up in the air rather than curving. When the stems of feather reed grass are broken by the wind or snow, they rest at odd angles against the remaining clumps. When falling snow settles along the length of the stems, the plants become winter sculptures that would be at home in a Manhattan art gallery.

To have a large selection of ornamental grasses highlighting your garden from spring to fall, be sure to temper your selection of cool-season grasses with plants that do well in summer heat and humidity. Most cool-season grasses flower early, but by surrounding them with later bloomers that include switch-grass *(Panicum virgatum)*, northern sea oats *(Chasmanthium latifolium)*, and fountain grasses, as well as the various annual grasses, you will have continuous bloom from spring to fall.

Types of Ornamental Grasses

One way of categorizing grasses is according to the particular environment to which they are best suited. Three distinct types are prairie grasses, woodland grasses, and grasses that prefer wet conditions.

▼ Prairie Grasses

When you think of an American prairie, you probably picture a vast, flat expanse filled with waving blades of grass. As the wind blows through this sea of grass, the billowing "waves" cast off seeds instead of spume.

For a meadow garden, or a prairie garden if you live in the Midwest, there are a vast number of grasses from which to choose.

Big bluestem *(Andropogon gerardii)* and little bluestem *(Schizachyrium scoparium)* both thrive in prairie gardens. Big bluestem reaches a height of 4 to 10 feet, grows quickly in hot weather, and does well in soils ranging from moist clay to dry sand. In late summer, the grass begins to turn a beautiful reddish copper color that gleams in the setting sun. Little bluestem is common throughout many areas in the Northeast and Southeast because it was commonly planted as a hedge against erosion by the Civilian Conservation Corps in the 1930s. Let it meander along a garden bank so its small, glistening flowers and reddish brown autumn color will be easily seen.

Ornamental grasses are ideal in naturalized meadow plantings. Neatly mowed pathways of lawn grass bring a sense of control and order to low-maintenance beds of grasses and wildflowers.

Canada wild rye *(Elymus canadensis)* bears bristly seed heads up to 9 inches long that bend under their own weight. The blue-green leaves look great in a garden border, but the plants are at their best when grown in large numbers.

Another popular prairie grass is switch-grass *(Panicum virgatum)*. Its open panicles look stunning against a dark background. Because they can grow up to 10 feet high, you can use these plants to make screens to block out unaesthetic aspects of the terrain.

Indian grass *(Sorghastrum avenaceum)* does well in almost any soil condition, and matures to bear flowers and seeds late in the season. The spikelets appear on 3-foot stems, bearing bright yellow anthers, which turn golden brown after the first autumn frost, when the foliage turns bright orange.

Other grasses for meadows and prairie gardens include northern dropseed *(Sporobolus heterolepis)* and prairie cordgrass *(Spartina pectinata)*, which spreads aggressively in its nonvariegated form.

▼ Woodland Grasses

For plantings next to the edge of a woodland, there are a number of sedges *(Carex* spp.*)* that take beautifully to moist soil in open shade. And don't overlook wild sedges like the plantain-leaved sedge *(C. plantaginea)*. High on the list of other desirable species for planting by the woods are northern sea oats, golden variegated hakone grass (especially beautiful when used as an edging), giant fescue, Bowles's Golden sedge, golden wood millet, bottlebrush grass, and tufted hair grass.

▼ Grasses for Bogs and Wet Places

Among the ornamental grasses that are capable of growing directly in water is the short-awn foxtail

For a waterside planting, try the tall, sword-shaped, grasslike leaves of variegated sweet flag (Acorus americanus *var.* variegatus), *planted here in direct contrast to blue hostas.*

(Alopecurus aequalis), a short perennial that is not really attractive enough for a formal bed or border, but is quite effective when used in waterside plantings. Another choice is cotton grass *(Eriophorum latifolium)*, which comes from North America and Europe. Cotton grass produces flowers that look like clean cottonballs on 16-inch stems, and dislikes hot climates. *Calamagrostis* species all grow well in shallow water or very moist soil.

Another water grass, wild rice *(Zizania aquatica)*, looks wonderful in a pool or pond, but will probably not produce enough grain for the table unless you devote most of the garden to its cultivation.

For underwater planting, try eelgrass *(Vallisneria spiralis)*, one of a small genus of grasslike aquatic herbs that are used in tropical fish tanks.

Noteworthy Cultivars

*B*esides the variegated grasses discussed on pages 32–34, there are other exciting cultivars in the grass world. In addition to looking for leaves with white or off-white variegations, you might want to seek out grass cultivars that have changed their typical green chlorophyll to a completely different color. Cultivars can also provide size variations; some are smaller than the species from which they were bred, and some are larger. In other cultivars the size of each individual leaf is different from the parent species. Occasionally, there will be a change in the flower itself.

One of the most beautiful color changes can be found in millet grass *(Milium effusum)*. The species is a perennial for shady woodland areas, about a foot high and a light greenish yellow color. The cultivar 'Aureum' is noted for its yellow leaves and flowers, a color that makes it a sparkling accent in shady locations with moist, fertile soil.

Possibly the most shocking color change involves Japanese blood grass *(Imperata cylindrica* 'Red Baron'). In late summer the leaves begin to trade their green chlorophyll for a blood red color that takes over more and more of the leaf surface as summer turns to fall.

Grass cultivars that are significantly different in size from the species allow gardeners to grow particular types of grasses in unexpected places. The charming annual hare's-tail grass *(Lagurus ovatus)* is usually about 2 feet high, but a diminutive cultivar called 'Nanus' seldom exceeds 6 inches in height and is ideal for rock gardens and containers.

A yellow cultivar of millet grass (Milium effusum 'Aureum') *is perfect when planted at the edge of a shady woodland.*

The exotic red color of Imperata cylindrica 'Red Baron' *makes it a garden favorite, especially when mixed with various perennials.*

Pampas grass (Cortaderia selloana) *can grow to 8 feet and is too large for many gardens. The cultivar 'Pumila', however, reaches only 5 feet and is perfect for the small border.*

The statuesque pampas grass *(Cortaderia selloana)* at its usual 8-foot height is too large for small backyards. But a new cultivar, 'Pumila', will be especially welcome because the ultimate size has been cut in half, to a mere 3 to 5 feet. The leaves of the cultivar are narrower, too; instead of being 1 inch wide like the leaves of the species, Pumila's leaves are just ½ inch wide. For gardeners with a space problem, Pumila is probably one of the most important grass cultivars in recent history.

A special cultivar of fountain grass, *Pennisetum alopecuroides* 'Moudry', has unusual flowers so dark in color, they are almost black.

In addition to the beautiful variegated purple moor grass *(Molinia caerulea* 'Variegata'*)*, there are two other *Molinia* cultivars to look for. 'Skyracer' grows 7 to 8 feet high, instead of the 2 to 3 feet attained by most other moor grasses. Another towering variety, 'Windspiel', is about the same height but has straighter seed stems.

Some cultivars are noteworthy primarily for differences in the width of their leaves. One of these, which is probably the finest and most useful cultivar of all ornamental grasses, is maiden grass *(Miscanthus sinensis* 'Gracillimus'*)*. Here the 1-inch leaf width typical of miscanthus has been reduced to a slim ¼ inch. The slender leaves give maiden grass a special grace.

Most of the cultivated hair grasses *(Deschampsia* spp.*)* are very valuable additions to the garden and have beautiful and airy flowers. One aptly named cultivar, 'Fairy's Joke', forms tiny plantlets on the flower spikes instead of flowers and seed heads.

Molinia caerulea *'Variegata' has creamy yellow-white stripes on a light green background. It makes a fine addition to any perennial border.*

The thin leaves of Miscanthus sinensis *'Gracillimus' form graceful fountains topped by the metallic sheen of the flowers.*

This cultivar has an unusual flower and the charming name of Deschampsia caespitosa *'Fairy's Joke'.*

Here Pennisetum alopecuroides *'Moudry' shows its late summer beauty with its attractive mounded form and unusual flowers.*

Grasses for Drying

Dried grasses are great additions to winter bouquets
and arrangements. Except for the seed heads of natal
grass *(Rhynchelytrum repens)* and squirreltail grass
(Hordeum jubatum), which shatter easily, the seed
heads of most ornamental grasses dry beautifully.

The only supplies you need for drying grasses are
some wire coat hangers, paper-covered twist-ties, and
a sharp pair of scissors.

Gather the grasses in midafternoon on a dry and
sunny day, after the morning dew has evaporated and
before the late afternoon damp sets in. Pick stems
with blossoms that are not yet completely open; once
picked most blossoms will continue to open, at least
for a day or two. Cut the stems so they are as long as
possible, because it's much easier to trim stems for a
short arrangement than to try to glue short stems
together for added length.

Strip away excess leaves, because they will only
shrivel. Tie small bunches of stems together, so that
air can pass easily between the seed heads. Hang the
bunches upside down on wire coat hangers, again
allowing plenty of room between bunches. Then hang
the hangers far apart in a room that is cool, dry,
dark, and airy. The cool temperature keeps the
remaining plant sap from drying too quickly and forc-
ing spikelets to go to seed; the dry and airy atmos-
phere prevents the formation of mold and mildew;
and the darkness forestalls premature fading of the
colored floral parts.

Remember to check your bunches every few days;
the stems will shrink as they dry, and stems that slip
out and fall to the floor could be ruined.

Most of the straight-stemmed grasses should be
dried in the above manner. Grasses with large and
weighty seed heads—like foxtail millet *(Setaria
italica)*, which has an attractive curved stem—should

Stems of big bluestem (Andropogon gerardii) *become a stunning fresh or dried arrangement in an attractive vase.*

be placed in a high-necked vase or container and kept
upright during drying. As with hanging bunches, put
upright grasses in a cool, dark, airy place to dry.

The leaves of many grasses, especially those of
Miscanthus species, are excellent additions to dried
arrangements, so be sure to save a few of them. Many
grasses are especially beautiful after they have been
touched by the first fall frosts.

When drying very delicate seed heads like those of
cloud grass *(Agrostis nebulosa)*, spray them lightly
with hair spray to help hold them together and keep
the heads from shattering.

Generally, your grasses will be ready to use in
arrangements in two weeks to a month.

1 *For a large vase like the one above, gather a good selection of ornamental grass plumes, cutting the stems as long as possible—they can always be trimmed later.*

2 *The final arrangement, fit to be the centerpiece of any table,* contains Pennisetum alopecuroides, Miscanthus sinensis, *and* Chasmanthium latifolium.

All miscanthus seed heads dry well, as do those of fountain grass, pampas grass, hair grass *(Deschampsia* spp.*)*, bottlebrush grass *(Hystrix patula)*, northern sea oats *(Chasmanthium latifolium)*, and switch-grass *(Panicum* spp.*)*. With the exceptions noted at the start of this section, most of the seed heads from annual grasses are also excellent for drying. Don't be afraid to experiment. You will probably find many more grasses in your garden whose seed heads are suitable for drying.

In addition, there are a number of other grasses whose dried leaves give off a pleasant fragrance. Especially fragrant are lemongrass *(Cymbopogon citratus)*, sweet vernal grass *(Anthoxanthum odoratum)*, and khus-khus *(Vetiveria zizanioides)*.

Many grasses are elegant when dried, especially annuals such as big quaking grass (Briza maxima) *shown here. The seed heads resemble puffed wheat and tremble in every breeze in the garden. Later they add grace and beauty to winter bouquets.*

Bamboos

*B*amboos are a subgroup of the grass family. The culms or stems of bamboo are very woody, and the plants have an extensive and well-developed system of rhizomes, which unfortunately always seem to have designs on other people's property. At the very least bamboos want to travel all over the garden.

Most bamboos are monocarpic—that is, they only live a short time after flowering. The tropical varieties tend to be more monocarpic than those in the temperate zone. Amazingly, all clones of a particular species of bamboo will flower at the same time regardless of where they are in the world.

There are bamboos hardy enough to survive in USDA zone 6 and even in zone 5, if they are given plenty of mulch and a sheltered place to grow.

Dozens of bamboos are offered for cultivation, but the following five favorites are good choices for American gardens.

Pygmy bamboo *(Arundinaria pygmaea)* is the smallest of the bamboos, usually reaching a height of about 3 feet, and in colder climates only 1 foot. It has a running habit and makes an excellent ground cover, especially in areas needing some kind of erosion control. When mowed, pygmy bamboos become more prostrate. The variegated form, *A. pygmaea* 'Variegatus', likes a shadier spot than the species.

The Kamurozasa bamboo *(Arundinaria viridistriata)* has velvety leaves striped in chartreuse, yellow, and pale green. The colors are best in the spring; then as summer turns to fall, the lighter shades disappear and the leaves remain a light green.

For a formidable hedge, there is the yellow-grove bamboo *(Phyllostachys aureosulcata)*, a species that reaches a height of 15 to 30 feet. It's the most winter-hardy of all the bamboos and can be used as a hedge, a screen, or a specimen plant.

Kuma bamboo grass *(Sasa veitchii)* is perhaps the most beautiful of all the bamboos. During the summer, the leaves are a dull green on plants usually about 3 feet high (but they can be taller in gentle climates). In autumn, the leaves wither and turn light brown around the edges, giving the plants a distinctly variegated aspect that lasts throughout the winter—a striking effect in the landscape. This species is hardy at least to USDA zone 7.

Heavenly bamboo *(Nandina domestica)* is a bamboo look-alike that is really a member of the barberry family from China and Japan. It's an attractive low-growing shrub that can reach 8 feet on occasion. The stems or canes are usually reddish brown and the leaves have a pink cast when new. Flowers appear in long panicles and are followed by colored berries that differ according to the cultivar, but are usually red. The plants are hardy to USDA zone 7, but will live in zone 6 with adequate winter protection.

▼ A Warning on Growth Habits

If bamboos interest you, read this cautionary note before you rush off to plant some. Bamboos are invasive. If you want a plant to take over your yard, then these are the plants to choose. But most gardeners wish to strike a happy medium and keep bamboo somewhat in bounds. When planting bamboo in the garden, be sure the roots are contained by a deep-set barrier (a *minimum* of 6 to 8 inches deep). Among the materials you can use to contain bamboo are concrete, stone, and metal edging. Or you can plant smaller varieties in pots set directly into the ground. If the plants get too big, mow them down with a lawn mower. After a time they will take the hint.

In the right setting, bamboos assume the status of small shrubs, but beware of their spreading beyond the allotted space. This garden combines bamboo with flowering perennials.

Other Grasslike Plants

E A R T H • W I S E
T I P

For a surprising look, try growing one of the water-loving grass look-alikes, such as umbrella plant (Cyperus alternifolius), among typical garden perennials. To supply the requisite watery conditions without drowning the neighbors, bury a small rubber or tough plastic cleaning pail (without the handle) in the border, fill it with water, and insert the umbrella plant. Make sure the umbrella plant is first planted in a slightly smaller pot.

*T*o the untutored eye, most of the following plants look like members of the grass family. But observe them at the right time of year and their prominent blossoms give them away. They are not true grasses, but grass look-alikes.

The sedges belong to the genus *Carex* and feature a surprising number of cultivars especially suited for shady spots in the border or the woodland garden. A special plant is *C. stricta* 'Bowles's Golden', which is notable for its lovely golden yellow color.

Sweet flag *(Acorus americanus)* was originally grown in Europe to extract a drug called calamus. Calamus imparts a pleasant smell to all parts of the plant, and when crushed between your fingers has a pungent, bitter taste. It has been used since the days of early Greece to treat diseases of the eye, to relieve flatulence and toothache, and as an ingredient in hair tonic. Until the strange flowers, which resemble the jacks in a jack-in-the-pulpit, appear, nobody would guess this plant is not a grass.

Sweet flag is beautiful in a small pond or water garden, and it is possible to grow the plant in a large submerged pot. The cultivar 'Variegatus' is much more attractive than the species; its creamy white-and-green-striped leaves add snap to the garden.

The grassy-leaved sweet flag *(Acorus gramineus)* is a smaller species that forms compact tufts, especially when grown at the edge of a pond. It was originally imported from Japan. The plant has a sculptural look, even though it is tiny (just 8 inches tall). Try a plant in a small pot. Keep the earth damp, and protect the plant from hot summer sun at noon.

Japanese or miniature sweet flag *(Acorus gramineus* 'Variegatus')* has flat, tough leaves striped with light green and white and arranged like miniature folding fans. It makes a marvelous houseplant and is attractive outdoors at the edge of a water garden where it can be seen up close.

Another group of grasslike plants—rushes—belongs to the genus *Juncus.* The common rush *(J. effusus)* is found growing wild in damp fields throughout the country. When brought into the garden, it becomes a very attractive plant, especially when in bloom. The flowers, although they are greenish brown, burst forth like tiny bubbles. Although this plant resembles a type of grass, the pointed spikes are really stems, not leaves, and the true leaves are tiny brown sheaths that cover the bottom of each stem. 'Spiralis' is a spectacular cultivar with green stems twisted just like a corkscrew.

Egyptian papyrus and the umbrella plant, which belong to the genus *Cyperus,* are especially beautiful in water gardens. The species *C. papyrus* can reach a height of 9 or even 10 feet; if that is too large for your backyard, there is a smaller cultivar, 'Nanus', that only reaches 3 feet. While not hardy, except in areas where the soil or water doesn't freeze, the plants are easy to keep over the winter in a warm garage or basement, as long as the roots are not allowed to dry out.

Bulrushes belong to the genus *Scirpus.* The banded bulrush *(S. tabernaemontani* var. *zebrinus)* is a striking plant that will get rave notices wherever it's grown. The pointed stems are horizontally striped with dashes of white on a green background.

Other grasslike plants are accustomed to growing in water or very damp soil. These moisture-lovers include horsetails *(Equisetum hyemale)*, such as the giant cultivar 'Robustus', which grows well over 6 feet. The narrow-leaved cattail *(Typha angustifolia)*,

Sedges, grasslike plants belonging to the Cyperaceae family, usually prefer damper and shadier conditions than grasses. Shown to the right is Carex stricta 'Bowles's Golden', with the orange flowers of avens (Geum reptans).

Although the above liriope (L. muscari 'Variegata') looks like a grass, it belongs to the lily family and produces decorative spikes of small blue-violet flowers in late summer.

Horsetails (Equisetum hyemale) have existed virtually unchanged since prehistoric times. They consist of tall jointed stems and minuscule leaves. Here, they add a great vertical element to lantanas.

51

Other Grasslike Plants CONTINUED

**Look-Alikes
That Are Lilies**

The lilyturfs are five species in the genus Liriope that are native to China and Japan and hardy in North America from zone 5 or 6 south. With their long, slender leaves they really look like grasses, but they belong to the lily family. They are perfect as ground covers or edging plants in moist, well-drained soil in open shade. Although evergreen, in colder climates (especially without snow cover) the leaves become quite tattered by mid- to late winter. Before the new leaves peek out, cut back the old leaves.

There are many cultivars, some with fine variegations. The spikes of purple flowers look like small violet hyacinths or like large grape hyacinths (Muscari spp.).

and its larger relative, the common cattail *(T. latifolia)*, also grow in water.

Every year in late spring, garden centers offer potted plant arrangements that contain brightly colored geraniums (usually zonal), a bit of ivy, and a green rosette of large, grasslike leaves stuck exactly in the pot's center. The leaves are tapered, about ½ inch in width and 1 foot long. It's difficult to believe that this grass is, in reality, a seedling of the cabbage palm *(Cordyline australis)*, a plant that can eventually become a 30-foot tree in its native New Zealand. If kept in a pot in your backyard, however, it will stay much smaller. Be sure to bring it indoors for the winter if the ground in your garden freezes.

There are two species in the genus *Phormium*, familiarly known as New Zealand flax. While only warm climates are hospitable to these plants, they are excellent in containers, or they can be moved to a temporary spot in the border for the summer months. The stiff and leathery leaves make striking foliage statements. *Phormium tenax* can have 9-foot leaves, and its five or six available cultivars offer a variety of leaf colors. For example, 'Variegatum' has leaves striped with creamy yellow and white, while 'Rubrum' has red leaves.

Mountain flax *(Phormium colensoi, or P. cookianum)* has leaves that reach about 7 feet and are greenish brown. It is easily grown from seed.

Turkeybeard *(Xerophyllum asphodeloides)*, also known as bear grass, is a native American plant. When the plant receives adequate snow cover or mulch and is planted in a protected spot, it will survive winter in zone 5—and it's worth the effort. The stiff, grassy leaves grow from a thick rootstock and are about 1½ feet long, making an arching fountain of

foliage. The surprise is in the flowering. From May to July, a 2- to 5-foot stem arises from the center of the grassy clump, bearing at its top a large and dense raceme of tiny white flowers.

Blue-eyed grasses *(Sisyrinchium spp.)* form a large genus of plants found growing as wildflowers across the country. If you walk through the fields in summer, you will always discover a few plants. At first glance you may think they are grasses that have suddenly learned the trick of producing flowers, but after investigation you will see that they belong to the iris family. Even the common name is misleading because the flowers are not always blue.

With blue-eyed grasses, as with daylilies, each blossom lasts but one day, although there are many buds on each flowering stem. Blue-eyed grasses look best in large groups in a naturalized area. They spread easily by seed.

Yellow-eyed grass *(Xyris arenicola*, or *X. torta)* looks exactly like a grass of small stature—its leaves are rarely longer than 16 inches—until it blooms with little thimblelike structures dotted with three-petaled yellow flowers. This is a delightful plant that will surprise garden visitors and is especially suited for a wild garden.

Regional Considerations

When choosing ornamental grasses for your garden, there are some regional factors that may come into play, depending upon where you live. For example, cool-season grasses must be grown in winter—or not at all—in hot, humid climates. If you plant grasses that can be invasive where winters are mild, they will run rampant and out of control.

Most ornamental grasses are harmless. However, if you live in a part of the country where the ground never freezes, some of the perennial grasses that are grown as annuals in the rest of the country can become invasive pests.

Natal grass *(Rhynchelytrum repens)* is often a problem in Florida. Feathertop grass *(Pennisetum villosum)*, another tender perennial widely grown as an annual, is troublesome in Florida and parts of southern California; another of the fountain grasses, *P. setaceum*, is always an invasive spreader when given the opportunity to roam.

Giant reed grass *(Arundo donax)* can be an aggressive perennial—and its large size can make it a formidable challenge. *Pennisetum alopecuroides* spreads, too, but not half as fast as its beautiful cultivar 'Moudry', a plant that self-seeds with frightening ease. Pampas grass *(Cortaderia* spp.*)* continues to spread throughout the warmer parts of the Southeast, as do a number of *Miscanthus* species.

And watch out for reed grass *(Phragmites australis)* and the narrow-leaved cattail *(Typha angustifolia)* when they get close to water, even in cooler climates. These plants are fine for a small pool, but do not plant them in an open area, where they will spread.

Not all ornamental grasses are hardy in the North, but several of the hardiest grasses do well in northern gardens where temperatures may fall to −30°F to −40°F in winter. Grasses that can take that kind of

Ribbon grass (Phalaris arundinacea *var.* picta) *is a tough grass that does well in cold climates, but it should be contained with an underground collar to prevent spreading.*

cold include giant miscanthus *(Miscanthus floridulus)*, hair grass *(Deschampsia* spp.*)*, porcupine grass *(Miscanthus sinensis* 'Strictus'*)*, blue oat grass, switchgrass, Indian grass, cordgrass (use the cultivar 'Aureomarginata', which has yellow-edged leaves), most of the *Festuca* species, and the beautiful little bluestem grass *(Schizachyrium scoparium)*.

Grasses for Containers

Small Grasses for Containers

Grasses of small stature will grow just as well in small pots as their cousins will in larger containers. The sedges, including all the Carex *species (except* C. pendula, *which is too large);* Cyperus *species; the smaller members of the genus* Juncus; *and even the smaller horsetails (*Equisetum *spp.) will do well if the soil is kept continually moist and plants are protected from hot sun.*

*A number of fescues (*Festuca *spp.), especially the various cultivars of* F. cinerea *and* F. amethystina, *look great in tiny pots. One cultivar of* F. scoparia, *called 'Pic Carlit', is only 3 inches high, and could easily win the neighborhood cuteness award in your garden.*

Years ago, during Victorian times, people grew grasses in all sorts of containers. In fact, a famous illustration of the time shows lawn grasses growing in pinecones, without any soil.

Old garden books describe placing a wet sponge in a glass bowl and then, on top, sprinkling grass seeds, which should soon sprout, to the amusement of all concerned.

Just about any grass will grow in a container if the container is large enough to support the final size of the grass and if the plants are properly watered, especially in the heat of summer. For example, if you live in the country, you might try growing field grasses in very decorative metal or clay pots.

Fountain grasses *(Pennisetum* spp.*)* have a neat and contained growth habit that makes the plants look good in containers, whether they are in flower or not. Annual fountain grasses (notably *P. setaceum* and its cultivars) are at their best when growing in contain-

ers, where the long, arching stems topped with the graceful seed heads can lean out into open air.

Most of the *Festuca* species, with their tufted form and appealing color, look good growing in small clay pots. A number of pots set on top of a wall or along the edge of a patio make handsome accents.

For a special look, grow Japanese blood grass *(Imperata cylindrica* 'Red Baron'*)* and blue oat grass *(Helictotrichon sempervirens)* in companion pots; the reds and the blues are very attractive together. If you live where the ground freezes in winter, bury the pots up to the rim over winter.

For larger patios and terraces, try taller grasses in large tubs or barrels. All of the *Miscanthus* species respond well to growing in containers—just be sure you allow enough room for them to spread.

The true annual grasses, especially the ornamental corns, also do well in pots.

Because they have fibrous roots, most grasses will do well in containers, as long as they are watered properly and fertilized on occasion. Here, potted grasses expand the boundaries of a small garden.

All of the bamboos thrive in containers, too, and planting them in containers is a good way to enjoy their beauty without worrying that the plants will spread. All *Carex* species do well in pots, too.

A variety of containers can be used to plant grasses. Almost anything that holds soil but also allows drainage is suitable, from old washtubs to discarded barrels, wooden kegs, wine casks, buckets, or metal or plastic horse troughs. Use an all-purpose potting mix that drains well.

Be sure to remember that unless a particular plant is best in the shade, most of the ornamental grasses need at least four hours of sun a day.

During winter months, especially where temperatures plummet, let perennial grasses go into dormancy. Unless the grasses are from the tropics, they must have at least a six-week period of cold (40°F or below) in order for them to grow the following year—and ultimately survive. Do not, however, leave containers without protection from alternate freezing and thawing, which kills the roots. Bury the pots in the garden, or put them in boxes and mulch around, between, and on top of the pots.

In addition to hardy grasses, you can put pots with a number of tropical species outdoors in summer, but they must spend winter in a warm spot. St. Augustine grass *(Stenotaphrum secundatum* 'Variegatum'*)* is a variegated form of a running grass that is often used as a lawn grass in the South and makes a welcome houseplant in the North, as long as it gets plenty of light. Basket grass *(Oplismenus hirtellus* 'Variegatus'*)*, originally from Africa, does beautifully in a hanging pot; the white-and-purple-striped leaves seem to sparkle in the sun.

The spreading qualities of Hakonechloa macra 'Aureola' are especially attractive when displayed in a well-designed pot.

Because of its stunning threadlike foliage, the weeping brown sedge (Carex flagelifera), a native of New Zealand, looks at home in containers. However, it's hardy only to USDA zone 7.

Meadow Grass Garden

*I*f you have a meadow on your property, you have the perfect place to experiment with a variety of ornamental grasses. Grasses are natural choices for the open landscape of a meadow that receives plenty of sun.

Since many grasses spread and fill in open areas, they quickly provide good cover, protecting the ground from soil erosion, particularly on hillside sites. Choose species that are native to your area or to a similar environment to ensure their long-term survival.

Plant List

1 Purple love grass
(Eragrostis spectabilis)
2 Porcupine grass
(Stipa spartea)
3 Tall moor grass
(Molinia caerulea var.
arundinacea)
4 Fountain grass
(Pennisetum alopecuroides)
5 Tufted hair grass
(Deschampsia caespitosa)
6 Porcupine grass
(Miscanthus sinensis
'Strictus')
7 Korean feather reed
(Calamagrostis arundinacea)
8 Ravenna grass
(Erianthus ravennae)
9 Silky-spike melic
(Melica ciliata)

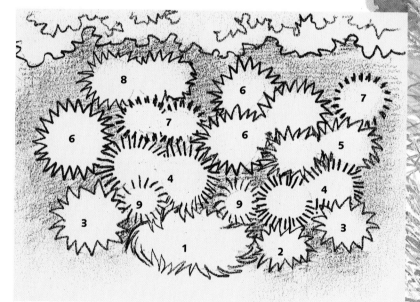

Porcupine grass (Miscanthus sinensis *'Strictus'), a form of eulalia grass, grows stiffly upright, often to a height of 6 feet. The common name allegedly derives from the horizontal yellow bands across the width of the leaf, which are said to look like the quills of an African porcupine.*

*Ravenna grass is a striking
accent plant. It sends up
showy plumes in the late
summer that can reach
heights of 12 feet.*

A Corner Garden of Grasses

The most attractive plant-ings often result from group-ing together several plants from the same species rather than a selection of plants from many different species. In this garden, the repeated use of lilyturf along the front and blue wild rye right behind it creates a strong and dynamic design. The repetition of form and color unifies the entire garden.

One of the benefits of gardening with grasses is that grasses can grow quite tall and provide privacy as well as beauty to any yard. This corner garden slopes from low border plants in the front to the 8- to 15-foot New Zealand flax in the back, which grows as a perennial in zones 9–10 and can be treated as an annual in cooler climates.

Experimenting with different grasses can be a sur-prise to most gardeners who think of grasses as just green foliage. In fact, the color combinations can be quite striking. Even more exciting is the discovery that as the season progresses, the grasses change colors, each species in its own way. This garden is mostly soft shades of blue and green in the summer, but gains striking hues of red, orange, tan, and brown in the fall. When you create a border of grasses, you're adding an ever-changing palette of color to the garden for you to enjoy throughout the growing season.

Plant List
1 New Zealand flax
(*Phormium tenax* 'Rubrum')
2 Variegated silver grass
(*Miscanthus sinensis*
'Variegatus')
3 Purple maiden grass
(*Miscanthus sinensis* var.
purpurescens)

4 Feather reed grass
(*Calamagrostis acutiflora*
var. *stricta*)
5 Fountain grass
(*Pennisetum alopecuroides*)
6 Crimson fountain grass
(*Pennisetum setaceum*
'Cupreum')
7 Japanese blood grass
(*Imperata cylindrica* var.
rubra)

8 Blue wild rye
(*Elymus glaucus*)
9 Big blue lilyturf
(*Liriope muscari*)
10 Yellow sedge
(*Carex elata*)

Fountain grass is one of the most popular true grasses for garden use. Its foliage sprays out, resembling a fountain that can rise several feet high. It does best in full sun and fertile, moist soil.

The crimson variety, Pennisetum setaceum 'Cupreum', is more sensitive to frost and should be grown as an annual in zone 8 and cooler.

Grasses for Wet Areas

*H*ere's a terrific way to turn a problem spot into a wonderful specialty garden. Take advantage of a natural wet area by creating a small pool or pond and surrounding it with a variety of grasses.

Using grasses in an area like this keeps the look natural, blending the pool into the surrounding landscape. Take a look around the area and try to incorporate existing features, such as boulders and stones and native plants that might already be in place.

Plant List
1 Grassy-leaved sweet flag
*(Acorus gramineus
'Variegatus')*
2 Giant reed
(Arundo donax)
3 Feather reed grass
(Calamagrostis acutiflora)
4 Umbrella plant
(Cyperus alternifolius)
5 Horsetail
(Equisetum hyemale)
6 Variegated manna grass
*(Glyceria maxima
'Variegata')*
7 Bulrush
(Scirpus cernuus)
8 Narrow-leaved cattail
(Typha angustifolia)

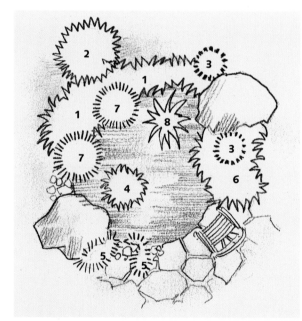

Native plants growing in the wild on public land are protected and may not be cut or dug up. This is particularly important in wetland areas. Be sure to purchase plants from reputable sources that propagate their own rather than collect from the wild.

Umbrella plant is a beautiful plant even when grown all by itself. It can be grown in a water garden or in a sunken tub filled with soil and water in a regular garden bed.

Bulrush is the common name for many Scirpus species, which are actually sedges, not rushes at all. Bulrushes are widespread in sunny wetlands and grow in dense stands, often together with cattails. They provide nesting cover for birds and other wildlife. Either plants or roots can be planted in shallow water or moist soil.

A Grassy Rock Garden

Bearskin fescue (Festuca scoparia) is a miniature mounding form of fescue. Considered an alpine grass, it forms low (4- to 6-inch) mounds of prickly foliage. These clumps can fill in the gaps next to rocks or larger plants.

*H*ere's a hillside rock garden featuring a collection of grasses, mostly low-growing mounded forms with flower spikes that bloom at different times throughout the spring, summer, and fall.

Start with a well-drained rocky slope and set a few flat stones for a path so that you can walk through the garden and see the plants up close. If you have existing boulders or rocks in place, count yourself lucky; if not, you can move rocks onto your site. Then choose your plants, placing taller plants in the back so that they can be seen against the sky. In this garden, the afternoon sun can be seen setting through the blue grama at the top—a spectacular sight!

Plant List

1 Blue-silver fescue
(*Festuca cinerea* 'Blausilber')
2 Blue fescue
(*Festuca cinerea*)
3 Blue fescue
(*Festuca ovina* var. *glauca*)
4 Blue hair grass
(*Koeleria glauca*)
5 Blue grama
(*Bouteloua gracilis*)
6 Bearskin fescue
(*Festuca scoparia*)
7 Variegated bulbous oat grass (*Arrhenatherum elatius* var. *bulbosum* 'Variegatum')
8 Lilyturf
(*Ophiopogon planiscapus* 'Ebony Knight')
9 Yellow sedge
(*Carex stricta* 'Bowles's Golden')
10 Orange sedge
(*Carex testacea*)
11 Variegated Japanese sedge
(*Carex morrowii* 'Variegata')

One of the reasons this garden is so striking is the use of a variety of colors and forms. Contrasting light and dark foliage and different plant shapes (weeping, spiking, or mounding, among others) add appeal and interest to the garden.

CHAPTER 2

Managing the Garden Environment

*O*rnamental grasses are essentially flowering perennials and annuals or other plants grown for their decorative foliage. As such, they need the same basic care that you would give flowers like daylilies or petunias, or foliage plants like hostas or coleus. • As you would other foliage plants, plant most grasses in early spring when the weather is still cool, although container-grown plants can go into the garden later in the season as well. • The hot weather of midsummer is not a good time to plant; if you must plant in the middle of summer, have plenty of water available so that the fibrous roots do not dry out. When buying plants by mail, have the grasses shipped in early spring or early fall to make sure the plants are not baked by summer heat on their way to you. Many of the cool-season grasses respond well to fall planting, which gives you a jump on having larger plants in next year's garden. In warmer climates grasses can be set out year-round.

Soil

There is a particular grass for every soil condition found in North America. For example, all the cultivars of fountain grass (Pennisetum alope-curoides), blue grama (Bouteloua gracilis), sweet vernal grass (Anthoxanthum odoratum), silky-spike melic grass (Melica ciliata), and purple moor grass (Molinia caerulea) will do well in acid soils, while big bluestem (Andropogon gerardii) and sideoats grama (Bouteloua curtipendula) are perfect for alkaline conditions.

Grasses that do well in sandy, dry soils include tufted hair grass (Deschampsia caespitosa), weeping love grass (Eragrostis curvula), and giant feather grass (Stipa gigantea).

When it comes to just plain poor soil, opt for blue grama, along with ribbon grass (Phalaris arundinacea var. picta), and members of the genus Festuca.

For heavy clay soils, choose feather reed grass (Calama-grostis acutiflora var. stricta) and tufted hair grass (Deschampsia caespitosa).

Grasses are not fussy plants, and some will grow if placed in a small hole in the earth and just given a little water. Most, however, produce the best leaves and flowers when provided with well-prepared soil. All you usually need to do is to amend the existing soil with organic matter such as compost or shredded leaves.

Most grasses, except those that do well in water, need good drainage. If your garden is on pure clay or solid rock, the best way to grow grasses is to build raised beds. Fill the beds with good topsoil mixed with plenty of compost.

If your garden has sandy soil, you will find that the soil drains quickly but has little ability to hold water. For the best results in sandy soil, choose drought-tolerant grasses, especially those adapted to seashore conditions. You can also begin to build up the soil by adding lots of organic matter each year.

It is important to check the soil pH when starting a new garden. There are specific grasses ideal for acid soils, and others that do well in alkaline soils. Your local county cooperative extension agent can provide information on soil testing.

To maintain soil for growing grasses, moderation is the key. While a little bit of a slow-release fertilizer (with a low nitrogen content) is fine for most of the larger species and cultivars, a running grass like ribbon grass *(Phalaris arundinacea* var. *picta)* will take off like wildfire if over-fertilized. See page 93 for more information on fertilizing grasses.

If you are growing grasses in a bed by themselves, you will probably want to mulch the bare earth between the individual plants. Use either long-lasting mulches like pine nuggets and pine needles, or choose shredded leaves, compost, or another mulch that will add to the fertility of the soil as it decomposes.

1 *To create a new island bed of ornamental grasses, first outline the bed on existing lawn with garden hose or rope. Adjust the shape until it pleases you.*

4 *Thoroughly work in the organic matter, crush any large clumps, then rake the surface smooth.*

2 *Once the outline is complete, remove the existing turf from the garden with a flat spade. Push the edge of the blade horizontally under the roots of the sod.*

3 *Break up the existing soil with a shovel, then add compost or composted livestock manure to enrich it. The improved soil will give the grasses the nutrients they need.*

5 *Set the plants, still in their pots, in the garden area. Shift them around until the composition looks right to you.*

6 *Plant, leaving enough space for the grasses to grow to their full size. Water thoroughly when planting is complete.*

Light

When asked to imagine grasses in nature, gardeners usually picture them growing under a bright sun and clear blue sky. Hundreds, if not thousands, of the grass species will indeed do their best when planted out in the open, where they are bathed in sunlight for most of the day. But just as there are some people who worship the sun, some who tolerate it, and some who actually shun sunlight, there are an amazing number of variations in light requirements among the ornamental grasses.

Generally speaking, grasses with variegated leaves need less sun than those with solid-color leaves. In most of the continental United States, most variegated plants will not stand up to the day-long direct rays of hot summer sun. In fact, many leaves with white areas (caused by a lack of chlorophyll) or tinted areas of colors other than green (created by colored chlorophylls) can easily burn in full sun. All of the variegated ornamental grasses and grasslike plants described in this book fit that description.

Although ornamental grasses generally like full sun, some will do quite well in partial shade. There are even a few woodland species that will survive in fairly deep shade, but they are not considered ornamental in form and are rarely used in gardens.

Except for gardens in the far North, most of the larger grasses, especially all the species of *Miscanthus* (including the variegated types), will grow with dispatch in less than full sun. Just three or four hours of sunlight a day is all they need, as long as the shade they receive the rest of the day is bright. A spot shaded by trees with small, lacy leaves, or with the lowest branches high off the ground, should provide a bright-enough setting.

When the larger ornamental grasses are planted in the deep shadows cast by buildings, walls, or thick trees, however, they are often slow to fill out their expected form. The leaf blades will droop and bend over. Trees that cause shade can be trimmed back to allow extra light to reach the plants. Where buildings create the shade, it's better to move the plants. Of course, floppy grasses can be propped up with stakes and garden twine. But the constant work needed for maintenance does not balance the unhappy look of a plant that is grown in an inhospitable place.

▼ Growing Grasses in Shade

Plants that thrive in shady conditions are always valuable. Lines of shrubs and bushes are often used to define spaces in landscape design, and low plants growing in the shade of the shrubs give the planting a finished look. Low plants are also useful to soften the edges of woodland gardens or shady pathways. Luckily, there are a number of grass species and grass look-alikes that are perfect for understory plantings.

Bear in mind that plants grown in shade need a little extra help with soil preparation. Because of the added stress on the root systems, make sure that any shaded areas of the garden have decent drainage. Unless a grass is specifically recommended for a damp or wet place, the soil should be loose and porous, with good drainage.

Most of the grasses and grasslike plants that will do well in shady spots are medium or small in size. A favorite ground cover in parts of the southeastern United States, the lilyturfs *(Liriope spp.)* have narrow leaves that stay green through much of the winter in mild climates, and they bear slender, dense spikes of

1 *The common shade garden may be attractive but is rather ordinary. With grasses, you can enhance the typical shade garden of hostas, ferns, impatiens, and begonias.*

2 *The addition of a few plants of Carex stricta 'Bowles's Golden' to the composition provides an unusual touch, and the yellow-green foliage brightens the look of the garden.*

Grasses for Shade

A few true grasses will do well in shade, including variegated maiden grass, bulbous oat grass, Festuca gigantea, Glyceria maxima *'Variegata', wild oats* (Chasmanthium latifolium), *tufted hair grass* (Deschampsia caespitosa), *bottlebrush grass,* Hakonechloa macra *'Aureola', and ribbon grass* (Phalaris arundinacea *var.* picta).

Among the best annual grasses for shade are cloud grass (Agrostis nebulosa) *and hare's-tail grass* (Lagurus ovatus).

Of the bamboos, kuma bamboo (Sasa veitchii) *will also adapt to shade, especially in the South.*

But most of the shade-loving plants are sedges—members of the genus Carex. *They include* C. buchananii, C. comans, C. stricta *'Bowles's Golden',* C. pendula, *and all forms of* C. morrowii. *Another good shade plant is Fraser sedge* (Cymophyllus fraseri).

tiny blue-violet flowers in summer. Cultivars with white flowers or variegated leaves are available. The beautiful golden variegated hakone grass *(Hakonechloa macra* 'Aureola'*)*, although slow to establish itself, is another good choice. Its soft, bamboolike leaves are a combination of green and golden yellow. Set plants the width of one plant apart. Both species of melic grass *(Melica altissima and M. ciliata)* are at home in partial to light shade and offer dramatic, arching flower heads in spring and summer.

If you are seeking larger grasses for a shady location, three come immediately to mind. Variegated silver grass *(Miscanthus sinensis* 'Variegatus'*)* tolerates partial shade and has long, narrow leaves striped in white and green. This grass looks wonderful next to other plants with white flowers. Bottlebrush grass *(Hystrix patula)* has bristly flower clusters that look like the narrow brushes used to wash out bottles. Sea oats *(Uniola paniculata)*, a dune grass that does best in full sun, will also perform reasonably well with a bit of shade.

Water and Grasses

Drought-Tolerant Grasses

Drought-tolerant grasses include blue grama (Bouteloua gracilis), wood grass (Sorghastrum avenaceum), wild oats (Chasmanthium latifolium), big bluestem (Andropogon gerardii), and because of its deep root system, switch-grass (Panicum virgatum).

But don't overlook most of the Miscanthus *species and cultivars; while they will not tolerate a complete lack of water, they will survive with reduced rations. Another ideal grass in dry conditions is prairie cordgrass (Spartina pectinata 'Aureo-marginata'), especially surprising since this grass also does very well in wet soils and even water.*

Water is used in the garden in two ways. First, it is necessary to keep plants alive, because even the toughest and most drought-resistant ornamental grasses must have *some* water to survive. And second, water is used as a decorative element in ponds, streams, or pools. Because of their graceful form, one of the best places to plant ornamental grasses is by the water's edge, where their usually massive yet supple forms can be reflected to double their beauty.

Since you will probably grow ornamental grasses in combination with other annuals and perennials in a garden bed or border, the best time to water is when the entire garden needs it. If you are new to gardening, ask your county cooperative extension agent for advice about the average amounts of rainfall you can expect in your area. That in conjunction with weather forecasts and your own awareness of garden conditions will tell you when it's best to water.

The traditional rule of thumb for watering is that gardens need an average of an inch of water per week. If you are lucky enough to get a good soaking rain every seven days or so, you will probably be able to ignore watering.

The best way to tell when the garden needs water is to stick your finger into the soil. If the soil feels dry a couple of inches below the surface, it's time to water. But remember that gardens with sandy soils, close to the sea, or in generally hot climates need more water than gardens in the northern parts of the country, where conditions are generally cooler and more moist. When you do water, it is important to water deeply in order to get grass roots to grow down into the soil, where they will be better able to survive hot, dry spells.

Because annual grasses live for only one season, they do not grow extensive root systems. Annuals like Job's-tears *(Coix lacryma-jobi)* or cloud grass *(Agrostis nebulosa)* do poorly when not supplied with enough water, and they need to be watered more frequently than perennial grasses.

There are a number of ways to get water to thirsty plants. Garden hoses and sprinklers that spray directly into the open air are the least efficient means, especially in areas of intense sun, high heat, and porous soil. Unfortunately, hoses and sprinklers are the only watering equipment most of us have. When you use sprinklers, remember to water early in the morning or late in the afternoon, or even at night if you must. Avoid watering at noon, when much of the water may evaporate before it reaches the plants. Try not to water on very windy days, again because too much of the moisture will evaporate.

For efficient watering, use soaker hoses. These special hoses have tiny holes that let water ooze slowly out to soak the ground, with little lost to evaporation. You can simply lay the hoses in the garden or cover them with mulch. More elaborate drip-irrigation systems use slender perforated plastic tubing connected with special couplings. Drip tubing can be installed underground or laid on top of the soil, and it can be connected to automatic timers on the top of the soil. Kits are available that provide all the needed parts.

Perfect drainage is not absolutely necessary for some grasses. A number of them will also do well in damp or wet soil, or even mud. And many—notably the sedges and rushes—prefer an evenly moist soil. Installing a plastic pool liner about a foot deep in some part of the garden will enable you to grow these moisture-loving plants next to other plants that would quickly expire in such conditions.

Many grasses are perfect for rock gardens, where their color and texture mix well with stone. Here, flowering blue oat grass (Helictotrichon sempervirens) *arches over a stony pathway in a dry location.*

Water and Grasses CONTINUED

Moisture-loving grasses can add texture, shape, and color to water gardens. Here, cattails, miscanthus, fountain grass, and other grasses combine beautifully with water lilies and lotus.

To install a plastic pool liner (as discussed on page 72), first lay out rope or garden hose to outline the shape you want your bog garden to be. Then excavate the hole to a depth of 1 to 2 feet. Remove any rocks exposed on the bottom or sides of the hole that might tear the liner. To make installation easier, make the bottom and sides of the hole as smooth and even as you can.

Unfold the liner and drape it into the hole. The heavy-gauge liners are heavy and bulky, so you will probably need an assistant for this step. Try not to drag the liner across the lawn or driveway—it could rip. The edges of the liner should overlap the hole; weight them down with bricks or stones.

Fill the hole with soil, water it to settle the soil, then add more soil. Repeat the procedure until the level of soil in the hole after watering is the same as the surrounding area. Cut off the excess liner, leaving a 6- to 12-inch edge. Cover the edge with soil, stones, or bricks.

Plant water-loving grasses, sedges, rushes, and flowers in the new garden. Water when necessary to keep the soil constantly wet.

It's surprisingly easy to grow water-loving grasslike plants in areas where they just don't seem to belong. Here's how to do it. Buy either plastic paint buckets or the more expensive rubberized plastic cleaning pails at a hardware or home-appliance store. Remove the handles, then sink the containers up to their rims in the soil in your garden. Plant a water-loving sedge, rush, horsetail, or other plant in a pot; set the pot directly in one of your buried pails; then fill the pail

Placed in a damp spot or a wet meadow, blooming cotton grass (Eriophorum latifolium) *becomes a drift of snow in the summer garden.*

with water. As the plant grows, the lip of the container will soon disappear. Don't forget to add water every few days to keep the pail filled.

A few true grasses will also thrive when grown directly in water. For example, *Calamagrostis* species, *Glyceria* species, *Spartina* species, and wild rice *(Zizania* spp.*)* all flourish in water. In many wet places along the East Coast, the common reed grass *(Phragmites australis)* does so well that it seems to hold acres of mud flats and areas of open water together.

But most of the grasses that will endure wet feet seem to prefer wet soil, mud, or boggy conditions, including all of the *Miscanthus* species, giant reed grass *(Arundo donax)*, and a host of the sedges *(Carex* spp.*)*. Horsetails *(Equisetum* spp.*)* grow well in wet soil, but will also do beautifully when placed in a pot, then submerged in a few feet of water. It is generally best to grow horsetails in pots because they spread rapidly in ideal conditions.

Although the plants described above like wet conditions, many other ornamental grasses, especially prairie grasses with deeply set root systems, will easily adapt to dry soils and less-than-perfect conditions. These grasses are so adapted to life subjected to water rationing that they can easily rot if their roots are left in water for any length of time.

This should be good news for gardeners who live in parts of the country where a general lack of rainfall is the rule and water is already—or will soon be—rationed. See the sidebar on page 72 for some grasses that can tolerate dry conditions.

Temperature Considerations

*I*n Chapter One we mentioned that some ornamental grasses (referred to as cool-season grasses) grow best in cool weather, while others are better suited to warm weather (and are considered warm-season grasses). Cool-season grasses like temperatures in the sixties or low seventies. They burst forth in late winter or very early spring, bloom some time in spring, and then grow slowly or go dormant during summer. When the temperature dips in fall, these grasses resume growing. In mild climates they may keep growing throughout the winter. When perennial grasses turn brown early in summer, it usually means they are cool-season grasses.

Sweet vernal grass *(Anthoxanthum odoratum)*, perennial quaking grass *(Briza media)*, *Calamagrostis*, sedges *(Carex* spp.*)*, tufted hair grass *(Deschampsia caespitosa)*, fescues *(Festuca* spp.*)*, blue oat grass *(Helictotrichon sempervirens)*, velvet grass *(Holcus lanatus)*, squirreltail grass *(Hordeum jubatum)*, bottlebrush grass, hair grass *(Koeleria* spp.*)*, melic grasses *(Melica* spp.*)*, golden wood millet *(Milium effusum* 'Aureum')*, *Phalaris*, moor grass *(Sesleria* spp.*)*, frost grass *(Spodiopogon sibiricus)*, and *Stipa* are all cool-season grasses.

Warm-season grasses thrive in heat, and grow best when the temperature is 80°F or higher. These grasses get started later in spring, then grow vigorously through the summer and bloom in late summer or fall. Many of them can be left standing to add interest to the garden all winter. The leaves of many warm-season grasses take on more color in fall. A good example is Japanese blood grass *(Imperata cylindrica* 'Red Baron')*, whose leaves turn blood red as summer fades to fall. The list of warm-season grasses includes *Andropogon* grasses, giant reed *(Arundo donax)*, grama *(Bouteloua* spp.*)*, wild oats *(Chasmanthium*

latifolium), pampas grass *(Cortaderia selloana)*, lemongrass *(Cymbopogon citratus)*, wild rye *(Elymus* spp.*)*, miscanthus grasses, moor grass *(Molinia caerulea)*, switch-grass *(Panicum virgatum)*, perennial fountain grasses *(Pennisetum* spp.*)*, little bluestem *(Schizachyrium scoparium)*, Indian grass *(Sorghastrum avenaceum)*, and vetiver *(Vetiveria zizanioides)*.

One way to consider the grasses that respond poorly to heat is to look at them as two-season ornamentals that provide garden color not once, but twice a season. Design the garden to feature them in spring and again in fall. Let annuals or summer perennials put on the show in hot weather. Some cool-season grasses will bloom in early spring, filling the garden with texture and color before most perennial flowers have begun to stir from their winter dormancy. Then in fall, when the summer perennials and annuals are ending their season, the cool-season grasses pick up again.

On the other hand, warm-season grasses will not even begin to grow until temperatures have heated up, the chill is gone from the soil, and nights are no longer cold. You can turn this potential drawback into an asset by planting warm-season grasses with other plants that reach their peak in spring. Spring bulbs such as daffodils, narcissus, and tulips make ideal companions. The bulbs provide an early garden display, and if you have planted them between warm-season grasses, as the bulb leaves brown and fade in late spring, the grasses will begin to grow and soon cover up the dying foliage of the bulbs.

Warm-season grasses also mix well with perennials that flower early in the season. In many borders, spring-blooming perennials such as globeflower, bleeding-heart, and primroses, as well as the Oriental poppies of late spring and wildflowers such as

Dozens of individual blue fescues (Festuca ovina *var.* glauca) *bring a carnival feeling and interesting geometry to this garden. Blue fescue does well in dry spots; damaged plants can easily be replaced and new plants quickly fill their allotted space.*

Virginia bluebells and Jacob's ladder, will put on a great surge of bloom only to quickly fade from the garden scene until next year. Here again, warm-season grasses can come to the rescue. As the weather warms they will quickly grow to cover the spots left vacant by the departing perennials. Their foliage can also serve as a buffer for strong contrasting colors of summer perennials and annuals growing nearby. And the soft rustling of their leaves in a passing breeze brings sound to the garden as well.

While a great number of ornamental grasses are hardy as far north as zone 4, many of the newer species and cultivars are best suited to zone 6 and warmer. When consulting nursery catalogues, check the hardiness ratings of each entry.

Bear in mind, however, that nurseries are not infallible when it comes to hardiness ratings. You may find that an experienced gardening neighbor will be able to offer more expert help than books and lists in determining which grasses will be hardy in your garden. And remember to check with your county cooperative extension office to see if they have a list of ornamental grasses that are hardy in your area.

Finally, remember that experimentation is often worthwhile. If a grass you want to grow is rated of borderline hardiness in your area, it is probably worth a try. You might even find that a grass listed as surviving only in the next zone south of your location will do quite well in a protected and well-mulched spot in your garden—perhaps in a bed on the south side of the house or garage, shielded from cold north winds. Understanding the microclimate in and around your garden will enable you to find sheltered spots in which you can experiment with grasses that would probably not survive in a more exposed location.

CHAPTER 3

Growing Grasses

*b*esides lichens and algae, grasses are the only plants found in the remote polar regions and the hottest deserts of the world. The next time you pass a construction site, where the worst soil imaginable has been piled in the hot sun, chances are you will see a few grasses starting to emerge. • But even though they are tough plants, grasses benefit from a touch of extra care when they are seedlings, when you plant them in the garden, and during the rest of the growing season. • For example, although many species can withstand long periods of drought, they do better in the garden if you give them ample water. • The great advantage of grasses is that they can be depended upon to grace a garden with foliage, flowers, and seed heads without really needing any coddling. Yet if you take a little care at the beginning, you will gain bigger and more beautiful plants.

Grasses from Seed

Starting grasses from seed allows you to grow varieties not available from nurseries. Moreover, seeds are considerably less expensive than plants.

In areas prone to late frost in spring, start seeds indoors, in a greenhouse, or in a heated cold frame. In areas with gentler climates, you can start most seeds outdoors directly (see pages 82–84).

Store seeds in a cool, dry place until you need them. If seeds must be stored for a month or so, place the packets in a tightly capped glass jar on a refrigerator shelf.

To germinate seeds, you will need a growing mix and containers to hold the mix. If you do not have a warm spot where temperatures are always above 65°F, use a soil-heating cable or mat.

Containers are manufactured of plastic, pressed peat, or pressed fiber. Seed-starting pots usually come in 2¼-inch or 3-inch widths and can be either round or square.

The growing medium should be lightweight and porous but retain moisture. A number of prepared mixes, mostly peat-based, are available. Commercial preparations are especially valuable because the messy mixing of ingredients has already been done, and the mixes are sterile when you buy them.

First, wet your growing mix by following the directions on the bag. If you are planting in peat pots, soak the pots in water before you use them. Next fill your containers, leaving about ¼ inch of space at the top; then pat down the mix.

The seed packets will tell you how deep to plant the seeds and whether light is needed for germination. If there are no directions, use these guidelines: cover seeds ⅛₆ inch or larger to the thickness of one seed; don't cover tiny seeds like those of cloud grass at all—just settle them in with a light spray of water.

Cover the containers of planted seeds with something to prevent the mix from drying out once germination starts. Plastic kitchen wrap or polyethylene bags work well. Remember to label each pot with the plant's name and the date of sowing.

If your seed-growing area is below 60°F, use a heating cable. Many grass seeds germinate most readily in damp, warm soil. If a heating cable is not practical, find a protected spot in the kitchen or bathroom.

When the first green shoots appear, move the containers into the sunlight or under a special lighting fixture used for seed flats. Remove the plastic covering to let in fresh air, and check on watering every day. When the mix starts to dry, carefully water the seedlings. Use room-temperature water; cold water could shock the tiny plants.

After the first grass leaves appear, begin using a dilute liquid fertilizer, especially if your growing mix does not contain added nutrients. Dilute the fertilizer to half the strength recommended on the package, and apply it only half as often as directed.

As the seedlings grow, move them to larger containers. If seedlings are still crowded, thin them out, leaving at least 1 inch between plants. Or prick them out and move them to individual pots.

To guard against damping-off, a fungal disease that attacks young seedlings, make sure you use a sterile potting mix and clean tools and containers when planting seeds. Also, be sure to provide good air circulation for seedlings.

1 To grow your own ornamental grasses from seed, first prepare a flat with a sterile commercial growing mix. The mix should be porous and well drained.

2 Thoroughly moisten the growing mix before placing it in the container. Scatter the seeds carefully over the surface of the moist mix.

3 Cover the seeds with a light dusting of the soil mix. Mist thoroughly with water to settle the seeds without dislodging them.

4 If seedlings become crowded, thin them out as necessary. When they are several inches high, as shown here, it is time to transplant them to larger individual containers.

TROUBLESHOOTING TIP

The pointed end of a clean knife, a plastic plant label, and even a sharpened tongue depressor are all excellent tools for transplanting seedlings. Insert the stick under the roots and lift gently. Carefully pick up the seedling by holding onto one of its leaves, move it to its new container, and lightly cover the roots with soil.

Planting Outdoors

Seedlings of most ornamental grasses have a tendency to look alike. And they are especially difficult to identify when growing next to weedy grasses from the field. So it's important that you transplant seedlings of perennial grasses to a well-prepared nursery bed that is kept scrupulously free of weeds, instead of just sticking them in empty spots in the garden. The plants should also be carefully labeled with the grass name and sowing date—it's remarkably easy to confuse them and forget which are which, especially when the plants are very young. When seedlings are 1 to 2 inches tall, thin them out to stand 6 to 12 inches apart, depending on their eventual height. Grasses that will eventually grow large will need the wider spacing.

If you are growing grasses in pots, make sure you move them to larger containers when the root systems begin to fill their present homes. Always prepare a new potting medium using bagged topsoil or landscape soil mixed with an equal volume of vermiculite,

perlite, or sharp builder's sand. Never use garden soil when growing grasses in pots that will eventually be moved indoor because the soil will not be porous enough and the pots will be too heavy. For growing seedlings that will be transplanted to the garden, you may find that plastic pots are better than clay. They are less expensive, easier to clean, and lighter to carry, and aesthetics are not a concern for pots that will hold plants only temporarily. Water potted plants regularly, especially as summer weather heats up.

Whenever possible, choose a cloudy day to transplant grasses to the garden. The sun quickly dries out soil, and on a sunny day, much of the water that you think is going to the plant is actually evaporating into the air.

It's important to dig a proper hole for any plant being moved to the garden. Although many ornamental grasses will survive being heeled into a slit in the garden soil, even if you leave them without water,

Mail-order nurseries often ship ornamental grasses in dormant, bare-root form. Get the plants into the ground as soon as they arrive and mulch well (if the soil has begun to warm) to conserve moisture.

Grasses and perennials are planted together in meadow and prairie gardens. Broadcast, or scatter, seeds of grasses, and annuals for first-year color, evenly over the area. Plug in perennial plants in succeeding years to fill empty spaces.

Planting Outdoors CONTINUED

they will lose a great deal of their strength with such cruel treatment. It will take days or even weeks for the plants to regain their vigor and begin to grow.

Dig a hole deep and wide enough to comfortably receive the plant. If your garden soil is not laced with plenty of organic matter, loosen the soil in the bottom of the hole and add some compost. Mix the compost into the soil, and scoop out the hole again if needed. Fill the hole with water, and wait for most of it to drain away.

Now remove the grass plant from the pot and examine the root ball. If the roots have started to wind around themselves, loosen them up with your fingers—it won't hurt the plant. Then set the plant in the hole so that the crown is at the same level it was when growing in the pot. Use your hands to firm up the soil around the plant. Water it again, then add some mulch.

If you must plant out very young grasses on a very hot day, make a sunshade by propping an old window screen up on sticks. Or lay a large pot on its side to provide needed shade as the new plant settles in.

▼ **Planting Annual Grasses**

Annual grasses love sun. Unless you garden in the South, where the noonday sun can be merciless (and where even annual grasses may do better with some shade), these plants want all the rays they can get. But, because annuals are programmed by nature to hurry through all their life functions in one season, they are not as picky about soil as perennials. This does not mean that you can freely plant annual grasses in bare rock or solid, baked clay, but you do not need to prepare the soil as thoroughly as you do to achieve optimal results with perennials.

In order to have a sequence of bloom throughout the summer, remember to start some seeds indoors in early spring, giving them plenty of light after germination to prevent leggy growth.

Most nurseries sell annual grasses just like annual flowers—as hardy annuals, half-hardy annuals, and tender annuals. Hardy annuals can tolerate some frost, so they can be planted directly outdoors at any time that the soil is workable. Half-hardy annuals can withstand some degree of cold, but not too much; you can plant them when the danger of heavy frost is past, although a light frost or two may still occur. Tender annuals are usually from tropical climates, so wait to plant them until all threat of frost is past.

A word of caution: As with perennial grasses, when sowing annual grasses directly into the garden, prepare and mark the seedbed with care; the new little plants look like any other grassy weed. Failing to mark their location can lead to confusion, perhaps the inadvertent loss of the plants.

As indicated earlier, when seedlings are 1 to 2 inches tall, thin them like perennials, leaving 6 to 12 inches between each plant, depending on their ultimate height. Wild oats (*Chasmanthium latifolium*), for example, should be kept 1 foot apart, while hare's-tail grass (*Lagurus ovatus*) needs only 6 inches of space between plants. Be generous with seeds when planting annuals—the smaller grasses look much better planted in substantial groupings than in small clumps or individually.

1 *Introducing grasses to a perennial bed, such as this one featuring rudbeckia and echinacea, adds interest without extra work.*

2 *Instead of edging the garden with low-growing flowers, plant a line of fescues.*

3 *You can also add some taller grasses, such as miscanthus, to bring vertical accents to the bed.*

4 *The ornamental grasses add variety to the bed, and it is still a low-maintenance garden.*

Buying Plants

*L*ike anything else in the plant world, you get what you pay for when you buy ornamental grasses from a nursery. Perennial ornamental grasses take at least three years to hit their growth stride. When you buy large, mature plants—usually sold in containers—they have been under the care of a nursery for a few years, and a great deal of time and effort has gone into their production. Therefore they are expensive. Smaller plants in 3-inch pots will eventually become specimen plants, but not for a couple of years. These small plants are much cheaper. When deciding which size to buy for your garden, you have to balance cost against the initial effect you want to achieve. If you can wait another two or three years for the plant to grow larger, a small plant is your best bet. But if you need the plant to have immediate impact, you will have to spend the money for a larger specimen.

Unfortunately, not all nurseries have their customers' best interests at heart. Be wary of small plants in large pots. Usually this means the plants have been potted up so that, if they are not sold, they can grow all season without repotting. You might wind up paying top dollar for a lot of dirt and very little plant. If you suspect this is the case, ask the salesperson to show you that there are plenty of roots on the plant.

Look for healthy plants with upright foliage and little sign of burning by the sun. This means they have been carefully watered. Don't buy variegated grasses, bamboos, and other such plants if they have been left out in the hot sun to bake.

Finally, make sure the plant is clearly labeled, with both the common and botanical names.

Local nurseries and garden centers usually put container-grown grasses on display when the time is right to plant them. Plants should be displayed in the sun or shade they need in the garden and should be labeled with botanical name, mature size, and growing conditions needed.

Planting Bamboos

*B*amboos do not have trunks; instead, they have culms, or hollow, jointed stems, that can grow very fast. Two kinds of bamboo are found at nursery centers. The first type is called sympodial or clumping bamboo; yellow-groove bamboo *(Phyllostachys aureosulcata)*, a relatively well-behaved plant, is a good example of this type. The second type is called monopodial or running bamboo; it is the kind that can run out-of-bounds. Monopodial bamboos are some of the most aggressive plants known to horticulturists. Their rhizomes spread in all directions, and each node or joint bears a single bud that can become a new bamboo. Pygmy bamboo *(Arundinaria pygmaea)* is an example of a running bamboo.

Running bamboos make beautiful ground covers, but before planting them, gardeners must take steps to contain them. A number of materials make effective barriers, including concrete blocks, metal edging sheets, and stone. But be warned, the barrier must extend from 2 to 2½ feet into the ground, or the rhizomes will simply grow under it. And joints must be sealed, or a wandering rhizome will find the opening and sneak through. Although paved driveways and roadways will restrict running bamboos, a surface concrete sidewalk will not. If you plant running bamboos next to a lawn, the runners can be kept in check with a lawnmower. When planting out larger bamboo species, some landscapers use 55-gallon steel drums as planters, completely burying them in the garden.

Consider light conditions when choosing a location for planting bamboos. Most green bamboos prefer full sun but will easily adapt to open shade in the South. Variegated bamboos should always be planted in light shade to prevent the leaves from burning.

Bamboos are tough plants, but they will grow more actively if a few guidelines are followed. First, give them reasonably fertile, sandy, lightly acid, well-drained soil—expecting them to excel in hardpan or pure clay is unrealistic. Second, transplant bamboos in late winter to early spring, and do not let uncovered roots dry out in the open air.

Finally, bamboos need plenty of water, so water them during spells of dry weather. For the most beautiful plants, fertilize in the spring with a formula rich in nitrogen such as 20-5-10, or with a high-nitrogen slow-release fertilizer, such as 18-6-12.

During the winter, bamboos become dormant and begin to lose leaves. Mulch the plants with the dead leaves, which have a high silica content, because bamboos need this chemical for active growth.

Bamboos need to be thinned as old culms die, usually in the fall. Cut off the old culm at ground level. Smaller bamboos should not be cut until they are at least three years old. When trimming a small bamboo, prune only the top, just above a node. Avoid severe pruning; the plants can suffer from this treatment.

Keeping Spreading Grasses in Bounds

The clumping types of ornamental grasses are usually not invasive because they slowly spread from the center out. However, if you want to cover an area of garden where an attractive grass would be an asset, consider planting one of the spreading grasses. Because they spread so easily, spreading grasses make perfect ground covers. Just remember that once established, spreading grasses are difficult—if not impossible—to control.

Ribbon grass *(Phalaris arundinacea* var. *picta)*, common reed grass *(Phragmites australis)*, and prairie cordgrass *(Spartina pectinata)* should be contained when planted, the same way as the running bamboos (see pages 87 and 89). Use metal curbing or concrete barriers to kept the roots from wandering.

Striped St. Augustine grass *(Stenotaphrum secondatum* 'Variegatum'), natal grass *(Rhynchelytrum repens)*, and basket grass *(Oplismenus hirtellus* 'Variegatus')* make beautiful houseplants or container speci-mens. But never plant these warm-climate beauties directly in a garden where the ground doesn't freeze, or they will spread with abandon and could become pests. Grow these plants as annuals in the North.

Weedy grasses include some annuals, such as squirreltail grass *(Hordeum jubatum)*, feathertop *(Pennisetum villosum)*, fountain grass *(P. setaceum)*, and *P. alopecuroides* 'Moudry'. Squirreltail grass, which becomes an aggressive spreader, is used to plant highway medians. Feathertop and fountain grass are major problems in parts of zones 9 and 10, and *P. alopecuroides* 'Moudry' is a minor threat from zone 4 south, seeding with a vengeance. All these annual grasses can be controlled by not allowing seeds to spread.

Bamboo spreads aggressively if not confined in a container or by an underground barrier. Here, bamboo canes have invaded the turf of a blue spruce.

1 *One way to confine the wandering rhizomes of bamboo is to plant it in a container. Here, black bamboo (Phyllostachys nigra) grows in a wooden planter.*

2 *Planting bamboos alongside a stream brings a decidedly tropical look to the garden, and the water keeps the bamboo from spreading, at least in one direction.*

3 *Another containment strategy is to surround bamboo with pavement. Here, Arundinaria viridistriata is kept in check by planting it within some paving blocks.*

Planting Grasses in Water

A few grasses, including *Glyceria* species, *Spartina* species, reed grass *(Phragmites australis)*, and wild rice *(Zizania aquatica)*, can be planted directly in water. Grasslike plants such as cattails, horsetails, and most of the sedges and rushes *(Juncus spp.)* will also grow in water. The problem with growing these plants is their tendency to invade. Cattails, for example, will speed up the process by which a small pond turns to dry land because, left unchecked, cattails soon turn into a solid sheet of plants. Cattails are attractive, but they will soon kill everything else in the pond if allowed to spread. Reed grass will do the same kind of damage.

If you want to grow any of these plants directly in water, plant them in submersible containers to keep them in check. If your water garden includes smaller plants in smaller pots, simply set them on top of sub-merged bricks or concrete blocks to bring them up to the correct level of the water, with the rim of each pot a couple of inches below the water surface. A good potting medium for a container placed in water is a blend of packaged potting soil and sharp builder's sand. Plants growing in submerged pots will usually do fine without additional fertilizer. If you do wish to fertilize them, wrap a small amount of granular all-purpose fertilizer in a piece of paper towel and push it into the soil in the pot.

One of the few grasslike plants to grow in shallow water without becoming a pest, and which is also effective in pots, is the soft rush *(Juncus effusus)*. The plant's thick and spiky silhouette is always welcome in the garden, but it is doubly effective when seen at the water's edge.

1 *Grasses are especially effective when planted near water. This water garden has maiden grass to the left and variegated miscanthus to the right.*

2 *Adding some small variegated grasses as an edging in front of the evergreens brightens the composition and introduces subtle color without being too distracting.*

Planting in Containers

When growing ornamental grasses in containers, drainage, soil content, watering, and pot size are all important considerations. If containers do not drain properly, the soil will soon become waterlogged and even grass roots will rot. Except for grasses that will grow directly in water, the potting medium must allow free passage of air to get oxygen to the roots, yet have enough organic content so that the soil does not dry out too quickly—especially in the hot sun.

The frequent watering needed for potted grasses causes nutrients to quickly leach out of the soil. The nutrients must be replenished regularly to keep plants healthy and vigorous, so use an all-purpose liquid fertilizer at least once every three or four weeks all summer with potted grasses. Follow package directions for diluting the fertilizer.

The soilless potting mixes used by nurseries are usually too light for long-term container growing. Instead, mix your own. Combine a good bagged potting soil, bagged topsoil, or plain garden soil that is reasonably fertile with an equal amount of sharp builder's (not beach) sand; you can also throw in a few handfuls of vermiculite. Avoid using only or too much peat moss; it is difficult to get wet and not really a good growing medium for grasses.

If you use a pot with a drainage hole, cover the hole with a piece of screening, a pot shard, or a bit of rock to keep the soil from coming out. (Do not plug the hole completely, or water will not be able to drain out.) Add enough mix to half-fill the container, position the new plant, fill in around it with more of the potting mix, and carefully firm the soil. Leave an inch of space at the top of the pot to make it easier to water the plant. Water well to help settle the soil around the new plant. If hollows develop, add more soil to level the surface. (See the photographs on page 92.)

Keep newly planted containers out of the hot sun for a few days so that the grasses can settle into their new home.

Hameln fountain grass (Pennisetum alopecuroides 'Hameln') does well in containers. A row of these plants can brighten up the edge of a patio or the top of a wall.

Planting in Containers CONTINUED

TROUBLESHOOTING TIP

Plastic pots are convenient to use and to store, but they are very light in weight and apt to blow over in strong wind. When you plant in plastic pots, either put them inside larger, more decorative pots or add some stones to the bottom of the pot to give added weight.

1 Before planting grasses in a container, line the bottom with pot shards or stones to provide some drainage. This is especially important for containers without drainage holes.

2 Prepare a light, porous potting mix containing soil; compost or a bit of peat moss, if you wish; and a lightening agent such as perlite or vermiculite.

3 Mix the potting ingredients thoroughly, and fill the tub with the mix to within an inch from the top. Water to settle the mix, and add more to bring up the level.

4 Plant the grasses, starting with the largest or tallest plant. When all plants are in place, water well and clip off any dead or damaged leaves.

Maintaining Grasses

Ornamental grasses are among the easiest of all garden plants to maintain. If you give them good growing conditions, they are undemanding and quite easy to care for. For watering needs and methods for watering grasses, see pages 72–75. Other aspects of grass maintenance, fertilizing and controlling pests and diseases, are considered below.

▼ Fertilizing

For the most part, ornamental grasses demand little in the way of fertilizing. In fact, over the long haul, all the prepared fertilizer in the world will not do as much good for your garden of grasses as properly prepared soil. Except for bamboos (see page 87), most of the ornamental grasses will perform beautifully if you lace your garden soil with compost or composted manure before you plant.

Another way to improve the quality of the soil is to use fresh compost as a mulch and till it into the soil at the end of each growing season to raise fertility values and organic matter content.

If you are starting a new garden or are in the early stages of a soil improvement program, the garden will probably benefit from some additional fertilizer, especially if you are growing grasses in combination with flowering perennials or other plants. An all-purpose liquid fertilizer will provide a quick nutrient boost and is easily applied. For a small garden, mix the solution in a bucket and pour it onto the soil around the base of the plants. For a larger garden, you may wish to purchase a special hose attachment that dispenses fertilizer as you water with the hose. Apply fertilizers sparingly; grasses on a rich diet may grow too vigorously and spread where you don't want them. For older grasses, as for seedlings, dilute liquid fertilizer to half the strength recommended on the package and apply it half as often as directed.

▼ Pests and Diseases

For ornamental grasses, the subject of pests and diseases can be covered in a few sentences. Grasses are among the healthiest plants in the garden. Occasionally some new growth may be nibbled by rabbits—or rarely slugs. Deer may also nibble on smaller grasses when they are hungry, but you can take protective measures as shown in the photograph on this page.

The only other problem is that in some areas of the country a fungal disease called rust may show up as orange spots or patches on the leaves. If you notice any leaves with these symptoms, remove them immediately. Burn them (if burning is permitted where you live) or seal them inside plastic trash bags and dispose of them with the household trash. Never put diseased leaves or any diseased plants on the compost pile, or you could spread the problem throughout the garden with next year's compost.

If deer are a problem in your garden, ornamental grasses like this tussock grass may be at risk in winter, when deer are hungry. If you cannot fence the perimeter of the property to exclude deer, enclose individual plants in chicken wire, plastic bird netting, or hardware cloth to protect them.

Weeding, Mulching, and Grooming

*P*eople who do not enjoy gardening often point to the job of weeding to make their case, calling it a dirty, backbreaking chore. Gardeners disagree, pointing out that weeding is one of the few jobs left where you can easily see where you began, know just how long it took to finish, and actually get a feeling of accomplishment when the work is done. For most gardeners, weeding is a soothing activity, an antidote to the stresses of a busy life. It offers a chance to spend time out in the garden among the plants.

Grasses sown directly in the garden need to be weeded when they are young, while they are still too small to mulch. Be sure to mark seedlings well, so that you are able to distinguish them from the young weeds that will inevitably pop up.

When your grass plants are big enough, by all means consider mulching them. Proper mulching accomplishes three things in the garden: it severely cuts back on the growth—and germination—of weeds; it helps to retain moisture in the soil by slowing the rate of evaporation; and when neatly spread, mulch makes the garden attractive, giving it a finished look. Mulching your ornamental grasses and grasslike plants will make them even easier to care for.

Various materials are available for mulching. You can choose according to your preference and the size of your pocketbook. Among the mulches found at garden centers are pine bark chips, marble chips, pine needles, pecan hulls, and cocoa bean husks (expensive but finely textured, and especially attractive if you like the smell of chocolate). There are also commercial mulches that include various mixes of organic materials, sometimes laced with aromatic cedar chips. Any one of these organic mulches is a good choice for

1 *Mulch bamboo with its own dried and fallen leaves to add necessary silica to the soil, to protect the roots, and to help retain moisture.*

ornamental grasses. Spread the mulch 1 to 2 inches deep, depending on its size—use the deeper layer for coarser materials like bark chips or pine needles.

Of course, peat moss and black plastic are also sold for use as mulch. Do not use peat moss; it is a poor mulch because it blows around when it is dry, and it actually repels water. Peat moss is most useful as a soil conditioner; work it into the soil to add organic matter and improve the texture rather than spreading it on top of the soil as a mulch. The use of black plastic is an aesthetic choice. Plastic does hold in water and cuts back on weed growth, but many gardeners hate the way it looks. If you like the effectiveness of black plastic but not its looks, you can always cover it with a more attractive mulch.

2 *Many grasses benefit from a mulch of wood chips, which keeps down weeds and conserves soil moisture. Fertilize with nitrogen when the mulch decomposes.*

3 *A mulch of carefully laid stones is attractive around grasses in a naturalistic bed or border, and can suggest plants growing in a dry riverbed.*

1 *Young grasses may benefit from staking or other supports, especially in windy locations. Firm the soil around the base of the new plant before setting supports in place.*

2 *A metal grid can support a young plant until it settles in and develops a strong root system. Use a bamboo stake and some twine when the plant grows taller.*

Thinning and Dividing

Clumping grasses, such as *Miscanthus* and *Pennisetum* species, grow out from the center, with the clump expanding a bit each year. After a number of years, the plants begin to look sparse in the center of the clump and require dividing. Warm-season grasses are best divided in late winter and early spring, while cold-season grasses can be divided either in fall or early spring.

Except for small fountain grasses and fescues, dividing grasses is hard work. You need a sturdy shovel, perhaps a crowbar for leverage, sharp shears, and a saw or ax to cut the clumps into sections of two or three plants. Cut out and discard the dead parts, then replant the still-vigorous sections. Cut back the foliage by about one-third to compensate for loss of moisture and for damaged roots.

1 When thinning bamboo, remember to wear gloves to prevent the leaves from cutting your hands.

1 To divide a crowded clump of grass, dig up the plant and rinse most of the soil from the roots so that you can see what you are doing.

2 Cut apart the clump so that each piece contains top growth and roots. Remove and discard any dead parts of the plant.

3 Cut back the foliage to make the divisions easier to handle and to reduce stress on the roots, then replant them in new locations.

Collecting and Saving Seeds

Saving seeds from ornamental grasses in your own garden is one of the best ways to increase your collection of plants and to build up a surplus of plants for trading with other gardeners.

In order to ensure germination, collect grass seeds when the plant's development is complete and the seeds are ripe. The best time to collect is usually when the seeds begin to fall away from the plant. Some grass species have a long hair, or awn, at the tip of each seed. When the awns appear is the best time to harvest seeds of those particular species.

Collect seeds by first clipping off the mature seed heads. Put the seed heads in a paper bag, and shake it to release the seeds, or hit the bag to knock out the seeds. You can also spread paper over a flat surface and pick out the seeds by hand. Don't worry—the paper will catch any seeds that fall.

Yet another way to collect seeds is to tie a paper bag over the seed head and leave it in place until the seeds drip into the bag. Shake the bag every couple of days to see whether the seeds have fallen.

Some wild grasses, including wild rye *(Elymus condensatus)*, wild chess *(Bromus secalinus)*, and green foxtail *(Setaria viridis)*, produce beautiful seed heads that are especially suited for the cutting garden and for dried bouquets. But the only way to grow these grasses is by collecting seeds from plants in the wild. They are rarely, if ever, offered by the trade.

Carefully discard any debris that is mixed with the seeds. The decomposition of this vegetable matter can cause seeds to rot before they germinate. Then store the seed in individual envelopes—small glassine envelopes sold by stamp collectors or #3 open-end paper envelopes for coins are perfect. Carefully write down the common name, the botanical name, and the date seeds were collected. Keep the packets in a cool, dry place away from excessive heat and moisture.

TIMESAVING TIP

Use a small hand lens (5x to 10x) to examine different grass seeds for their natural beauty. Sizes vary from the very tiny seeds of love grass (Eragrostis spp.) *to the plumed excesses of the fountain grasses* (Pennisetum spp.) *to the beadlike seeds of Job's-tears* (Coix lacryma-jobi), *which are often used to make jewelry.*

For grasses that have seeds with awns (long hairs at the tip), collect seeds when the awns are fully formed.

End-of-Season Activities

As early in the spring as the weather allows, cut back all the clumps of ornamental grasses to just a few inches above the ground. Now the new season's growth will appear fresh and green—without ragged and broken reminders of last year's grasses.

Unlike most perennials, many ornamental grasses keep up the garden show until well into winter. The farther south your garden is located, the longer the grass plants will remain in good shape. In autumn, the grasses turn varying shades of beige, tan, gold, and brown, and they will remain that way until cut down by winter weather or your clippers next spring. In fall and winter, the grass garden becomes more sculptural, with the plants standing as sentinels in the garden in a palette of soft, neutral colors.

In the North, winter winds will eventually shatter the seed heads, break the stems, and tatter the foliage of the now-dry grasses—although they will last well into winter in most places. In warm climates, warm-season grasses are likely to stand up all winter long, and cool-season grasses will often grow actively or at least remain green throughout the season.

No matter where you live, when summer is at an end, go through the grass garden and look for any broken stems and dead leaves. Trim off tattered, messy leaf tips, and entirely remove all the damaged or dead stems and leaves. Take the plant debris—as long as it is not diseased—to the compost heap.

If you live where winters are severe enough that dry grasses seldom last long in good condition, cut back all the plants to within a few inches of the ground.

Make sure grasses are well watered going into winter. When the ground freezes the grasses will not be able to take up any more moisture through their roots until spring.

Autumn is a good time to mulch perennial grasses to neaten up the border or to add protection for grasses that are growing near the limit of their hardiness range. Winter mulches are also useful in locations where mild spells are likely to cause the frozen soil to thaw before refreezing in a cold spell. Such

1 *Cut back large grasses, such as miscanthus, once a year at the beginning or end of the growing season.*

1 *When the ground begins to freeze in fall, spread loose mulch such as bark chips, shown here, around and between plants to a depth of at least 2 inches.*

2 *Use hedge clippers or pruning shears to cut back all the stems to within a few inches of the ground.*

3 *The clipping removes unsightly old foliage and makes room for fresh new growth to take its place.*

**E A R T H • W I S E
T I P**

For extra protection in winter, it's a good idea to add an extra inch or two of mulch on top of what's already there in your garden. If winter winds blow some of your mulch off the garden, replace it as soon as you can. If necessary, cover the mulch with boards or tarps to keep it in place.

2 *Pine needles are a good mulch for plants that prefer an acid pH, such as the* Carex comans *shown here. Spread them 3 or 4 inches deep.*

alternate periods of thawing and freezing often make the soil heave and buckle, and the dormant roots of perennials can be forced right out of the ground. Once exposed, they are likely to be killed by prolonged exposure to cold temperatures and drying winds. The purpose of a winter mulch in this type of garden is to keep the soil frozen during mild spells to prevent heaving.

When the ground begins to freeze, spread a layer of shredded leaves, shredded bark, or other loose material at least 2 inches deep, tucking it closely around the bases of your perennial grasses.

Check under the mulch periodically over the winter to make sure no roots have been heaved out of the ground. If you find any exposed roots, gently push them back into the ground and cover them with soil.

Regional Calendar of Ornamental Grass Care

 Spring   ☀ Summer

COOL CLIMATES

Spring

- Cut last year's grasses back to the ground if you have not already done so.
- In early spring, start seeds indoors for annual grasses.
- Begin fertilizing indoor seedlings when the first leaves appear.
- Plant out cool-season grasses when danger of heavy frost is past.
- Plant and transplant warm-season grasses when the soil warms and all danger of frost is past.
- Thin direct-seeded grasses when plants are 1 to 2 inches high.

Summer

- Weed grasses until they grow about 6 inches tall, then mulch to conserve soil moisture and keep down weeds.
- Plant container-grown grasses whenever weather conditions are not too stressful.
- Water grasses that are not drought tolerant during spells of dry weather. Check water levels of plants in containers.
- Cut grasses for arranging or drying when flowers or seed heads appear.
- Remove seed heads from weedy grasses before seeds drop.

WARM CLIMATES

Spring

- Plant and transplant warm-season grasses when the weather settles.
- Thin direct-seeded grasses when plants are 1 to 2 inches high.
- Weed grasses until they grow about 6 inches high, then mulch to conserve soil moisture and keep down weeds.
- Plant container-grown grasses whenever weather conditions are not too stressful. Provide some afternoon shade for new transplants.

Summer

- Water grasses that are not drought tolerant when needed. Check water levels of plants in containers.
- Cut grasses for arranging or drying when flowers or seed heads appear.
- Remove seed heads from weedy grasses before seeds drop.
- Renew mulches that become thin over summer.
- Plant cool-season grasses in late summer or in early fall.

Fall

- Collect, clean, and store seeds of wild grasses and other grasses when seeds ripen.
- Work decomposing organic mulches into the soil to improve its quality, or dig fresh compost into the soil.
- Cut back any broken stems and dead or damaged leaves to keep plants neat as the growing season comes to an end.
- Divide crowded, overgrown clumping grasses.
- Mulch grasses of borderline hardiness before ground freezes.
- Pull and compost annual grasses.

Winter

- If alternate freezing and thawing is likely during winter in your area, mulch perennial grasses after the ground freezes.
- In late winter or early spring, cut last year's grasses back to the ground before new growth begins.
- Update garden plans; design new grass plantings.
- Order seeds and plants early for best selection.
- Make sure you have all the supplies you will need on hand for starting seeds.

This table offers a basic outline of garden care by season. The tasks for each season differ for warm and cool climates: warm climates correspond to USDA plant hardiness zones 8 through 11, and cool climates to zones 2 through 7. Obviously, there are substantial climate differences within these broad regions. To understand the specific growing conditions in your area, consult the zone map on page 127. Also be sure to study local factors affecting the microclimate of your garden, such as elevation and proximity of water.

- Plant cool-season grasses in early fall.
- Collect, clean, and store seeds of wild grasses and other grasses when seeds ripen.
- Work decomposing organic mulches into the soil to improve its quality, or dig fresh compost into the soil.
- Pull and compost annual grasses.
- Cut back broken stems and dead or damaged leaves.
- Divide crowded, overgrown clumping grasses.

- Cut last year's grasses back to the ground before new growth begins.
- Update garden plans; design new grass plantings.
- Order seeds and plants early for best selection.
- Start seeds indoors for cool-season grasses to plant out in late winter or early spring.
- Begin planting cool-season grasses in late winter if weather is mild.

Ornamental Grasses for American Gardens

*T*his section provides concise information on more than 115 ornamental grasses recommended for American gardens. The plants have been selected on the basis of beauty, adaptability, and availability. If you're looking for grasses for particular uses—of a certain height, for instance, or with variegated foliage—look first at the Height and Spread and Ornamental Features columns. If you need plants for a shady spot, look at the Growing Conditions column. Or you might prefer to look at the photos, read the descriptions, and then decide which grasses will grow well in your location. Each photograph shows a species or variety described in the entry.

▼ About Plant Names

Plants appear in alphabetical order by the genus name, shown in bold type. On the next line is the most widely used common name. The third line contains the complete botanical name: genus, species, and where applicable, a variety or cultivar name. If a species is known by two names, the second will appear in parentheses below the first.

Common names vary, but botanical names are the same everywhere. If you learn botanical names, you'll always get the plant you want from a mail-order nursery or local garden center. If you request hair grass, for example, you might be sold *Deschampsia* or you could be sold a species of *Koeleria*. To get the kind of hair grass you want, you need to know its Latin name.

When several species in a genus are similar in appearance and cultural needs, they are listed together in a single entry in the chart. In the case of a genus containing two or more species or varieties that are quite different from one another, or that are easily confused, each of the recommended species or varieties is given a separate entry in the chart.

The second column of the chart provides a brief plant description. Look here to see if the plant is tall, clump forming, mounded, or creeping.

▼ Height and Spread

In this column you will find the range of height the grass can attain, including its flower, and also the area over which the plant will spread at maturity. It is important when planting ornamental grasses to allow enough space for them to grow to their full size.

▼ Ornamental Features

This column describes the features that make the grass desirable for gardens. If you are looking for a grass to use as a specimen, ground cover, or one whose flower heads are good for cutting and drying, check this column first.

▼ Hardiness Zones

Plant hardiness is generally an indication of the coldest temperatures a plant is likely to survive. But many plants also have limits to the amount of heat they can tolerate. In this chart hardiness is expressed as a range from the coolest to the warmest zones where the plant generally thrives. The zones are based on the newest version of the USDA Plant Hardiness Zone Map, shown on page 127.

▼ Growing Conditions

The last column of the chart summarizes the best growing conditions for the plant. Look here for information on the plant's light, moisture, and soil requirements.

		Height & Spread	Ornamental Features	Hardiness Zones	Growing Conditions
ACORUS SWEET FLAG *Acorus americanus*	*A wetland perennial of the arum family whose 2- to 4-ft., swordlike leaves have a single rib. Both the leaves and the 1- to 3-in., coblike cluster of yellow-green flowers are fragrant. One cultivar has yellow-striped leaves.*	Height: 3–6' Spread: 1–2'	*Dense clusters of tall irislike leaves. Fragrant flowers in late spring to late summer.*	4 to 11	*Full sun to partial shade. Sweet flag grows best in wet or waterlogged soil or in shallow ponds, but adapts to upland soils, except those that dry out completely. Plants may benefit from division of the rhizomes every several years.*
ACORUS GRASSY-LEAVED SWEET FLAG *Acorus gramineus* ◀ *A. gramineus 'Variegatus'*	*A wetland perennial whose stiff, narrow leaves form grassy tufts. This species lacks the fragrant foliage and flowers of its taller relative sweet flag. The leaves of 'Variegatus' are striped white; a dwarf cultivar is also available.*	Height: 8–18" Spread: 6–8"	*Dense tufts of grass-like leaves. Flowers in summer.*	6 to 11	*Full sun to partial shade. This plant grows best in wet or waterlogged soil or in shallow ponds, but adapts to upland soils, except those that dry out completely.*
ALOPECURUS YELLOW FOXTAIL GRASS, MEADOW FOXTAIL *Alopecurus pratensis* 'Aureus'	*A perennial grass whose cylindrical flower clusters form a foxtail 1–2½ in. long. Bright golden yellow, ¼-in.-wide, 6-in.-long leaves grow in erect clumps. Each leaf has a green midrib.*	Height: 1–2' Spread: 6–18"	*Striking yellow foliage. Flowers in spring. Use as a meadow grass in eastern U.S.*	6 to 9	*Full sun to light shade. Moist, well-drained soil. Plants grow most vigorously in cool weather. They do poorly in excessively drained soil and hot situations. This is a non-invasive species that spreads slowly by runners.*
AMMOPHILA AMERICAN BEACH GRASS *Ammophila breviligulata*	*A native dune-building grass of the Northeast and Great Lakes. This tufted perennial has stiff, green, 1-ft.-long leaves and creeping, sharp-pointed rhizomes that enable it to spread. Yellow cylindrical flower clusters are borne on tall stems.*	Height: 2–3½' Spread: 2–3'	*Dune-building grass. Attractive summer flower clusters persist into winter.*	4 to 7	*Full sun. Well-drained, sandy soil with even moisture. Plants need frequent sand deposition and protection from foot traffic to continue to grow vigorously. This is an ideal dune plant for coastal areas north of the Carolinas.*
ANDROPOGON BIG BLUESTEM *Andropogon gerardii*	*A bold, clump-forming, perennial grass native to the tallgrass prairies. Blue-green leaves take on bronze and red tones in late summer as purple flower spikes rise above the foliage. The 3- to 5-branched seed head resembles a turkey's foot.*	Height: 4–10' Spread: 1½–3'	*Meadow grass with good late summer color. Attractive flower heads and seed heads; use in dried arrangements.*	4 to 10	*Full sun. Grows best in well-drained, moist soil, but tolerates clayey soil and drought once established. Propagate by seed or by clump divisions in spring. Bluestem does most of its growing during the warm season.*

◀ *Indicates species shown*

Ornamental Grasses for American Gardens

		Height & Spread	Ornamental Features	Hardiness Zones	Growing Conditions
	ANDROPOGON BROOMSEDGE BLUE-STEM *Andropogon virginicus*	*A perennial grass that forms small tufts with most leaves overlapping on lower third of stem. Often the flower head resembles a small whisk broom with bronzy sheaths and 1-in. white flowers clustered at the top of the stem.*	Height: 2–3' Spread: 1–2'	*Meadow grass with sepia color in autumn. Flowers in late summer. Use attractive flower and seed heads in dried arrangements.*	3 to 11	*Full sun. Sandy, nutrient-poor soil is ideal, but broomsedge grows well in a wide variety of conditions, from wet to dry. It can be a bit weedy in disturbed sites.*
	ANTHOXAN-THUM SWEET VERNAL GRASS *Anthoxanthum odoratum*	*A perennial whose soft, fragrant evergreen leaves are $\frac{1}{3}$ in. wide and 6–8 in. long. Cylindrical clusters of light green flowers rise 12–16 in. above the clumps of foliage, turn golden tan in summer, and persist into autumn.*	Height: 1–2' Spread: 8–15"	*Cut or bruised leaves exude pleasant aroma. Flowers in late spring to early summer.*	5 to 10	*Full sun to light shade. Fertile, humus-rich, moist, well-drained soil. This cool-season grass can adapt to many conditions, but does not grow well where summers are hot and dry.*
	ARRHEN-ATHERUM BULBOUS OAT GRASS *Arrhenatherum elatius* var. *bulbosum* 'Variegatum' (*A. bulbosum* var. *variegatum*)	*A clump-forming perennial grass with chainlike, bulbous rootstocks at the base of its green-and-white-striped foliage. The flat leaves are $\frac{1}{4}$ in. wide and 6–12 in. long. The shiny, silvery green flowers have twisted bristles.*	Height: 1–2' Spread: 6–12'	*Meadow, rock garden, or border grass. Variegated foliage. Flowers in late spring to early summer.*	4 to 9	*Full sun to partial shade. Fertile, moist, well-drained soil. Oat grass grows best in cool weather; avoid hot, dry situations. Plants slowly spread by runners. Cut back in summer to stimulate autumn growth.*
	ARUNDINARIA PYGMY BAMBOO *Arundinaria pygmaea* *A. pygmaea* 'Variegatus'	*A small, slender-stemmed bamboo with bright green, branching canes that are purple at the joints. The fuzzy, bright green leaves are 5 in. long and $\frac{3}{4}$ in. wide. 'Variegatus' has creamy-white-striped leaves.*	Height: 6–12" Spread: 1–2'	*Ground cover or erosion-control grass. Colorful, low-growing bamboo shoots.*	7 to 11	*Full sun to partial shade. Average soil. Once established, pygmy bamboo is relatively drought tolerant and can withstand shade. It may spread aggressively, so provide root barriers where needed. Mow every several years to rejuvenate.*
	ARUNDO GIANT REED *Arundo donax* *A. donax* var. *variegata*	*A large, bold perennial that is the commercial source of reeds. Stems emerge from deep, woody rhizomes and bear feathery flower and seed heads above light blue-green, 3-in.-wide, 1- to 2-ft.-long leaves. Variegata has white-striped leaves.*	Height: 6–25' Spread: 4–8'	*Screen or specimen plant, especially for wet areas. Bold shoots create a dramatic bamboolike effect. Beautiful flower heads in late summer to late autumn; use for arrangements.*	6 to 10	*Full sun. Moist, humus-rich soil. This fast-growing, warm-season grass may become weedy with time.*

			Height & Spread	Ornamental Features	Hardiness Zones	Growing Conditions
	BAMBUSA OLDHAM BAMBOO *Bambusa oldhamii* COMMON BAMBOO ◄ B. vulgaris	*Large, clump-forming bamboos with round, 4-in.-thick stems and dense 6- to 10-in. leaves. B. oldhamii has green stems that are white below the joints. B. vulgaris is uniformly green.*	B. oldham. Height: 15–25' Spread: 5–10' B. vulgaris Height: 20–60' Spread: 10–25'	*Screens and architectural accents. Dense foliage.*	B. oldhamii 9 to 11 B. vulgaris 10 to 11	*Full sun to light shade. Evenly moist, humus-rich soil. Plants may become massive with time.*
	BOUTELOUA SIDEOATS GRAMA *Bouteloua curtipendula* BLUE GRAMA ◄ B. gracilis	*Delicate-looking natives from the East to the Great Plains chiefly valued as forage for livestock. Pearl-like fruits on one side of the stem (B. curtipendula) or in arching combs (B. gracilis) make them handsome garden plants.*	B. curt. Height: 12–32" Spread: 1–2' B. gracilis Height: 8–24" Spread: 6–12"	*Excellent rock garden and meadow grasses. Flowers in late spring to early summer; use in dried flower arrangements.*	B. curt. 4 to 9 B. gracilis 3 to 10	*Full sun. Well-drained, fertile soil. These are warm-season perennial grasses that withstand drought, heat, cold, and even mowing once established.*
	BRIZA BIG QUAKING GRASS ◄ Briza maxima LITTLE QUAKING GRASS B. minor	*A genus of grasses grown for the graceful way the showy, heart-shaped spikelets shake in the breeze. B. maxima has ¹/₂- to ³/₄-in. flower heads. Both B. minor and B. maxima are annuals that turn golden brown.*	B. max. Height: 1–2' Spread: 6–8" B. min. Height: 4–16" Spread: 4–6"	*Flowers in late spring to late summer. Use attractive flower and seed heads in fresh or dried arrangements.*	Hardy annual	*Full sun. Average, moist, well-drained garden soil. Sow B. maxima directly in the garden in early spring; sow B. minor in mid-spring.*
	BRIZA PERENNIAL QUAKING GRASS Briza media	*A decorative clump-forming perennial grass whose pyramidal clusters of bright green, heart-shaped flowers rise above the foliage and turn tan in the summer. The lush, soft, 1-ft.-long leaves are evergreen.*	Height: 1–2' Spread: 10–15"	*Ground cover or rock garden grass. Flowers in mid- to late summer. Use attractive flower and seed heads in fresh or dried arrangements.*	4 to 10	*Full sun. Fertile soil with ample moisture, especially while the grass is becoming established; thereafter, it is more drought tolerant. Plants will spread slowly and self-sow.*
	BROMUS ERECT BROME ◄ Bromus erectus MEDITERRANEAN BROME B. lanceolatus (B. macrostachys)	*Flat-leaved grasses that bear narrow clusters of dark red flowers. B. erectus is a perennial with upright shoots and 4- to 8-in.-long flower clusters. B. lanceolatus is an annual with sparse clusters of coarsely bristled, 1-in. flowers.*	B. erectus Height: 2–3' Spread: 6–12" B. lanc. Height: 1–2' Spread: 6–8"	*Erect, tufted foliage. Red to purple flowers in summer. Use striking flower heads in dried arrangements.*	B. erectus 5 to 9 B. lanc. Hardy annual	*Full sun. Fertile, moist, well-drained soil. Sow B. lanceolatus seeds where desired in mid-spring.*

◄ *Indicates species shown*

Ornamental Grasses for American Gardens

		Height & Spread	Ornamental Features	Hardiness Zones	Growing Conditions
BUCHLOE BUFFALO GRASS *Buchloe dactyloides*	A sod-forming perennial native to short-grass prairies. It has curly, 1/10-in.-wide, 2-in.-long, gray-green leaves and short flower shoots. The foliage turns lavender in autumn and tan in winter.	Height: 2–8" Spread: 6–12'	Meadow, turf, or lawn substitute. Attractive foliage throughout the year, regardless of moisture conditions.	3 to 9	Full sun. Well-drained soil; clay loam is best. Once established, buffalo grass is heat and drought tolerant. Plants spread slowly. Separate male and female plants.
CALAMA-GROSTIS FEATHER REED GRASS *Calamagrostis acutiflora* var. *stricta*	A large ornamental grass that forms tight vertical clumps. Feathery panicles of yellow flowers appear in spring, deepen to gold by autumn. The foliage of this perennial is evergreen where winters are mild but turns tan elsewhere.	Height: 4–6' Spread: 6–12"	Versatile meadow, specimen, or screen grass. Flowers in mid- to late spring. Seed heads remain standing above foliage through winter.	5 to 9	Full sun to very light shade. Moist soil; roots should be kept moist throughout the growing season. Plants tolerate clay soils but not drought. This is a fast-growing but noninvasive grass that grows best in cool weather.
CALAMA-GROSTIS FOXTAIL GRASS, KOREAN FEATHER REED *Calamagrostis arundinacea* var. *brachytricha* ◄ *C. arundinacea* 'Karl Foerster'	Erect, clump-forming perennial grasses with fluffy flower plumes. C. a. brachytricha has large pink flower clusters in late summer. 'Karl Foerster' has reddish bronze flowers in late spring.	C. a. brach. Height: 1–4' Spread: 1–2' 'K. Foerst.' Height: 1–4' Spread: 1–2'	Background, accent, or specimen grasses. C. a. brachytricha flowers in late summer, 'Karl Foerster' in late spring. Use attractive flowers in fresh or dried arrangements.	5 to 9	Full sun to partial shade. Well-drained soil with even moisture. Both varieties will withstand heat if moisture is available, but neither is very drought tolerant. C. a. brachytricha is the more shade tolerant of the two. Both spread slowly by runners.
CALAMA-GROSTIS BUSH GRASS *Calamagrostis epigejos*	A coarse perennial with extensive creeping rhizomes that produce erect tufts of 1/3-in.-wide, 1-ft.-long, pale green leaves. Dense, erect clusters of feathery, pale purple flowers are several inches wide and 1 ft. long.	Height: 2–7' Spread: 6–12"	Background, accent, or specimen grass. Attractive flowers in late summer; use in fresh or dried arrangements.	4 to 7	Full sun. Average soil. In the East the species has become weedy, invading sandy soils, salt marshes, fields, and disturbed places.
CAREX NEW ZEALAND SEDGE *Carex comans* 'Bronze Form' ◄ *C. comans* 'Frosty Curls'	Grasslike perennials with solid stems and leaves in threes. C. comans has fine, narrow, evergreen leaves growing in dense tufts. The leaves of 'Bronze Form' are a bronzed tan; the curly leaves of 'Frosty Curls' have white tips.	Height: 10–18" Spread: 10–18"	Tufted border, container, or edging plants. Dense flowering spikes atop attractive foliage in late spring to mid-summer.	7 to 9	Full sun to partial shade. Moist, fertile soil. Streamsides are ideal, but sedge will adapt to upland situations as long as soil never completely dries out. Plants may be short-lived.

		Height & Spread	Ornamental Features	Hardiness Zones	Growing Conditions
	CAREX VARIEGATED SEDGE *Carex conica* 'Variegata'	A clump-forming evergreen sedge with 1/4-in.-wide, deep green leaves edged with white. It is sometimes sold as *C. conica* 'Marginata'.	Height: 3–12" Spread: 3–6"	Rock garden, container, or edging plant; makes an attractive low ground cover.	5 to 9	Partial sun to shade. Moist, fertile soil. This sedge adapts to upland situations as long as soil never completely dries out. Cut tops back to 3 in. in early spring to encourage vigorous growth.
	CAREX VARIEGATED JAPANESE SEDGE *Carex morrowii* 'Aureo-variegata' ◀ *C. morrowii* 'Variegata'	Clump-forming sedges with stiff, arching, pointed evergreen leaves striped silvery white in 'Variegata' and creamy yellow in 'Aureo-variegata'. The foliage is 1/3 in. wide and 15–20 in. long.	Height: 8–18" Spread: 1–2'	Ground cover, specimen, massing, or container plants. Variegated foliage.	5 to 9	Full sun to partial shade. Moist, fertile, slightly acid soil. Light shade is ideal, but these sedges adapt to sunny situations as long as soil never completely dries out.
	CAREX PALM SEDGE *Carex muskingumensis*	A sprawling sedge, native to the Great Lakes, with leaves that are arranged like miniature palm fronds. The drooping, light green leaves turn yellow with the first frost.	Height: 2–3' Spread: 2–3'	Ground cover, container, or water garden plant. Feathery, palmlike foliage.	4 to 9	Full sun to partial shade. Moist, fertile soil. Streamsides are ideal; plant will grow in shallow water or upland sites if soil never completely dries out. It grows best in cool weather, self-sows, and spreads slowly by underground runners.
	CAREX DROOPING SEDGE, WEEPING SEDGE *Carex pendula*	A sedge with leathery, dark green leaves up to 3/4 in. wide, arching in a tuft. Graceful, arching flower stems bear drooping, pendulous flowers in late spring, lasting all summer. The plant is semievergreen or evergreen in mild climates.	Height: 2–4' Spread: 2–3'	A focal point, specimen, or accent in beds and borders. Unusual drooping flowers.	5 to 9	Partial to light shade. Moist soil. This sedge thrives near shady streams or in moist woods. It does best in cool weather, coming back early in spring. This slow-growing species self-sows and will spread.
	CAREX YELLOW SEDGE *Carex stricta* 'Bowles's Golden' (*C. elata*)	A sedge whose springtime tufts of bright yellow, 1/3-in.-wide leaves with light green edges deepen to a more uniform green later in the season. Dark brown flowers are borne on spikes above the foliage.	Height: 1–2' Spread: 2–3'	Ideal for massing at water's edge. Bright clumps of yellow foliage in spring; evergreen through winter.	5 to 9	Full sun to partial shade. Moist, fertile soil. Streamsides are ideal; plant even grows in shallow water. Yellow sedge will adapt to upland situations as long as soil never completely dries out.

◀ *Indicates species shown*

Ornamental Grasses for American Gardens

		Height & Spread	Ornamental Features	Hardiness Zones	Growing Conditions
CAREX ORANGE SEDGE *Carex testacea*	An evergreen, clump-forming sedge with gracefully arching, $1/16$-in.-wide, 1- to $1\frac{1}{2}$-ft.-long leaves. The foliage emerges olive green in spring and turns orange with age. The flowers are very small.	Height: $1–1\frac{1}{2}'$ Spread: 1–2'	Ground cover for moist sites. Container plant. Flowers in late spring.	8 to 9	Full sun to partial shade. Moist, fertile soil. Streamsides are ideal, but orange sedge adapts to upland situations as long as soil never completely dries out. Plants may be short-lived.
CAREX TEXAS SEDGE *Carex texensis*	A low, spreading sedge native to the Southwest. The lustrous evergreen leaves are very slender and grasslike. This sedge can withstand foot traffic and even be mowed as a substitute for conventional lawns.	Height: 3–4" Spread: 6–12"	Ground cover, lawn, or edging between stones in walkways. Flowers in early spring.	7 to 10	Full sun to partial shade. Moist, well-drained, fertile soil. Mow periodically to encourage vigorous growth.
CAREX FOOTHILL SEDGE *Carex tumulicola*	A clump-forming sedge with arching, lustrous, dark evergreen leaves that are $1/8$ in. wide and 1- to $1\frac{1}{2}$- ft. long. The leaves have brownish bases and grow from a tough, creeping rootstock.	Height: 10–15" Spread: 10–15"	Meadow grass or ground cover (even under trees). Flowers in spring.	8 to 11	Full sun to partial shade. Moist, fertile soil is ideal, but this sedge adapts to upland situations once it is established. One of the more rugged, drought-tolerant sedges, it grows moderately fast.
CHASMAN-THIUM WILD OATS, NORTHERN SEA OATS *Chasmanthium latifolium*	A streamside native, related to coastal sea oats. Its clumps of $1/2$- to $3/4$-in.-wide, 4- to 6-in.-long leaves turn coppery in autumn and brown by winter. Attractive flattened clusters of 1-in. green flowers turn tan as they mature.	Height: 2–5' Spread: 1–2'	Meadow or rock garden grass. Attractive foliage texture and colors. Flowers in late summer. Flowers and fruits effective in fresh or dried arrangements.	5 to 9	Full sun to partial shade; plants need even moisture if grown in full sun. Deep, humus-rich, moist soil. This self-sowing native grass grows best in warm weather.
COIX JOB'S-TEARS *Coix lacryma-jobi*	A perennial that resembles corn in having 1- to 2-ft.-long, $1\frac{1}{2}$-in.-wide, flat leaves and tassels of male flowers at the tip of the stem. Female flowers produce beady, $1/2$-in., gray, white, or black fruits. Variegated cultivars available.	Height: 3–6' Spread: 1'	Massing or specimen grass. Flowers in summer. The bony fruits can be used for beads.	9 to 11	Full sun. Moist, well-drained soil. This evergreen grass is grown as a perennial in zones 9–11, an annual elsewhere. Start seeds indoors in late winter, and transplant outdoors in early to mid-spring. Soak seeds overnight to speed germination.

			Height & Spread	Ornamental Features	Hardiness Zones	Growing Conditions
	CORDYLINE CABBAGE TREE, GRASS PALM *Cordyline australis*	An evergreen palm that reaches tree size as a perennial but is often grown as an annual grass, with clumps of sword-shaped leaves 1–3 ft. long and 1–2 in. wide. Bronze or variegated leaved cultivars are available.	Height: 20–30' (smaller as a container plant) Spread: 1½–4'	Specimen or accent plant in warm climates; foliage container plant elsewhere. Flowers late spring to frost.	9 to 11	Full sun to partial shade. Fertile, humus-rich, well-drained soil is best. Once established it is quite drought tolerant.
	CORTADERIA PAMPAS GRASS ◀ *Cortaderia selloana* *C. selloana* 'Gold Band'	A genus of very large, clump-forming perennials with separate male and female plants bearing long, evergreen, 1-in.-wide leaves. Flower shoots rise several feet above the foliage. C. selloana 'Gold Band' has green-and-gold variegation.	Height: 8' Spread: 4'	Specimen or hedge grass. Attractive variegated foliage. Flowers in late summer; use for fresh or dried arrangements.	8 to 11	Full sun. Moist, well-drained soil; withstands dry soils once established. Pampas grass grows best in warm weather. Cut back and thin every several years to keep it growing vigorously.
	CORTADERIA DWARF PAMPAS GRASS *Cortaderia selloana* 'Pumila'	A dwarf cultivar of pampas grass that, despite its small stature, is one of the most floriferous cultivars. Female plants have much showier, creamy ivory flower plumes than males. The gray-green leaves are ½ in. wide and up to 3 ft. long.	Height: 3–5' Spread: 3–5'	Specimen or hedge grass. Attractive gray-green foliage. Showy flowers in late summer; cut for fresh or dried arrangements.	6 to 10	Full sun. Moist, well-drained soil; withstands dry soil once established. Pampas grass grows best in warm weather. Cut back and thin every several years to keep it growing vigorously.
	CORTADERIA PAMPAS GRASS *Cortaderia selloana* 'Sunningdale Silver'	One of the largest of the pampas grass cultivars. It needs a lot of room to display its 1- to 2-ft.-long, feather-shaped, creamy white flower plumes.	Height: 6–10' Spread: 6–10'	Specimen or hedge grass. Attractive variegated foliage. Showy flowers in late summer; cut for fresh or dried arrangements.	7 to 10	Full sun. Moist, well-drained soil. One of the sturdiest cultivars, 'Sunningdale Silver' withstands both winds and dry soil once established. It prefers warm weather. Cut back and thin every several years to keep it growing vigorously.
	CYMBOPOGON LEMONGRASS *Cymbopogon citratus*	A tender perennial grass whose leaves are a commercial source of lemon oil. The bright evergreen leaves, ½–1 in. wide and 2–3 ft. long, grow in dense clumps and are used extensively in Southeast Asian cooking.	Height: 3–6' Spread: 2–3'	Pot herb or ornamental clump-forming grass. Bright green leaves. Flowers in late summer.	9 to 11	Full sun to light shade. Moist, well-drained, humus-rich soil. Lemongrass grows best in warm weather and is drought tolerant once established. Grow it as an annual north of zone 9, sowing seeds or planting rootstock divisions in mid-spring.

◀ *Indicates species shown*

Ornamental Grasses for American Gardens

			Height & Spread	Ornamental Features	Hardiness Zones	Growing Conditions
CYPERUS UMBRELLA PLANT *Cyperus alternifolius* PAPYRUS *C. papyrus*	Grasslike perennials of the sedge family whose somewhat triangular stems are topped by whorls of leafy bracts that surround clusters of light brown flowers. The bracts of umbrella plant are 4–12 in. long and those of papyrus are 1–1½ ft. long.		C. altern. Height: 1–4' Spread: 3–5' C. papyrus Height: 4–9' Spread: 3–7'	Lush accents for moist and aquatic gardens. Can be grown as container plants. Flowers in summer.	9 to 11	Full sun to partial shade. These plants require soil that is constantly moist or submerged in water.
DACTYLIS VARIEGATED ORCHARD GRASS *Dactylis glomerata* 'Variegata'	A variegated dwarf form of a tufted, evergreen perennial grass of meadows and barnyards. The soft, flat, ¼-in.-wide, 10-in.-long leaves are striped with silver and green. The flowers are gathered together in pea-sized clusters.		Height: 1–2' Spread: 6–18"	Meadow or border grass. Variegated foliage. Flowers in mid- to late spring.	4 to 9	Full sun to light shade. Dactylis grows in rich or poor soil as long as it is well drained and evenly moist. It grows best during cool weather and can be aggressive. 'Variegata' may revert back to all-green leaves with time.
DESCHAMPSIA TUFTED HAIR GRASS *Deschampsia caespitosa* *D. caespitosa* 'Fairy's Joke'	Tufted perennials with clusters of shiny, 2-flowered spikelets with hairlike projections giving them an airy appearance. 'Fairy's Joke' bears tiny plantlets among the flowers at the top of the plant.		Height: 1–4' Spread: 1–3'	Border or naturalizing grasses. Interesting plantlets among the flowers in late spring. Use cut flowers for fresh or dried arrangements.	4 to 9	Full sun to full shade; partial shade is ideal. Moist, well-drained, slightly acid, humus-rich soil. Moisture is essential for good growth of this cool-season grass. Avoid sunny, droughtlike situations. Plants often self-sow.
DESCHAMPSIA TUFTED HAIR GRASS *Deschampsia caespitosa* 'Bronzeschleier'	A cultivar whose name 'Bronzeschleier' is German for "bronze veil," referring to the yellow-bronze color of the flowers. These grow in 2½- to 3-ft. clusters that arch over and nearly obscure the light green foliage.		Height: 1–4' Spread: 1–3'	Border or naturalizing grass. Delicate haze of flowers in spring to early summer; cut for fresh or dried arrangements.	4 to 9	Full sun to full shade; partial shade is ideal. Moist, well-drained, slightly acid, humus-rich soil. Moisture is essential for good growth of this cool-season grass. Avoid sunny, droughtlike situations. Plants often self-sow.
DESCHAMPSIA TUFTED HAIR GRASS *Deschampsia caespitosa* 'Goldstaub'	A cultivar named 'Goldstaub', or "gold dust," for its golden yellow flowers. The 1- to 2-ft.-long panicles of flowers are borne above tufts of medium green foliage.		Height: 1–4' Spread: 1–3'	Border or naturalizing grass. Delicate haze of flowers in spring to early summer; cut for fresh or dried arrangements.	4 to 9	Full sun to full shade; partial shade is ideal. Moist, well-drained, slightly acid, humus-rich soil. Moisture is essential for good growth of this cool-season grass. Avoid sunny, droughtlike situations. Plants often self-sow.

			Height & Spread	Ornamental Features	Hardiness Zones	Growing Conditions

| | **DESCHAMPSIA** SCOTLAND TUFTED HAIR GRASS *Deschampsia caespitosa* 'Schottland' | One of the most robust cultivars of D. caespitosa. It has dark green, 2- to 3-ft.-long leaves and 1- to 2½-ft.-long clusters of flowers. | Height: 2–4' Spread: 1–3' | Border or naturalizing grass. Delicate haze of flowers in late spring to early summer; cut for fresh or dried arrangements. | 4 to 9 | Full sun to full shade; partial shade is ideal. Moist, well-drained, slightly acid, humus-rich soil. Moisture is essential for good growth of this cool-season grass. Avoid sunny, droughtlike situations. Plants often self-sow. |

| | **ELYMUS** EUROPEAN DUNE GRASS, SEA LYME GRASS ◁ *Elymus arenarius* CANADA WILD RYE *E. canadensis* | Densely tufted perennials with bold spikes of flowers that resemble domesticated rye grass. Sea lyme has long, rigid leaves and smooth flowers. Wild rye has broad leaves and bristly flower spikes. Both are available in blue-leaved forms. | E. aren. Height: 6–48" Spread: 6–24" E. canad. Height: 2–5' Spread: 1–4' | Ground cover, naturalizing, or erosion-control grasses. Bold flowers in mid-spring to midsummer. | E. aren. 4 to 10 E. canad. 3 to 8 | E. arenarius, full sun; E. canadensis, full sun to light shade. Moist, well-drained soil. E. arenarius can be aggressive, but tolerates salt spray and grows well as a dune stabilizer in coastal areas. |

| | **ELYMUS** GIANT WILD RYE ◁ *Elymus condensatus* *E. condensatus* 'Canyon Prince' | A Pacific Coast native with dense tufts of robust semievergreen leaves. The 8- to 12-in.-long, branching clusters of blue-green flowers turn yellow-tan as they mature. 'Canyon Prince' is considered to have the finest blue foliage and flowers. | Height: 5–10' Spread: 3–6' | Ground cover, naturalizing, or erosion-control grass. Attractive flowers in late spring; use in fresh or dried arrangements. | 8 to 10 | Full sun to light shade. Moist, well-drained, sandy soil. Plants may go dormant during midsummer in hot, dry situations; prolong growth by supplying additional moisture. They are drought tolerant once established, and can be used as dune grasses. |

| | **ELYMUS** BLUE WILD RYE *Elymus glaucus* | A semievergreen wild rye with dense clumps of smooth, erect, blue-green, ½- to 1-in.-wide, 1- to 2-ft.-long leaves. Velvety green, 4- to 6-in.-long clusters of flowers are borne on spikes above the foliage. | Height: 1–4' Spread: 1–3' | Dense ground cover, meadow, or rock garden grass. Flowers in late spring to early summer. | 3 to 9 | Full sun to light shade. Moist, well-drained soil. Plants may go dormant during midsummer. Provide more shade in hot climates. This species starts to grow in late winter or early spring. |

| | **EQUISETUM** COMMON HORSETAIL, COMMON SCOURING RUSH *Equisetum hyemale* | An evergreen perennial more like a fern than grass, with a hollow, jointed stem. The light green color deepens during winter. Spores are produced in a conelike structure at the top of the plant. | Height: 1–4' Spread: 1–3' | Ground cover and filler for moist sites. Attractive, dramatic stems. | 4 to 10 | Full sun to partial shade. Wet, humus-rich soil; will grow well in water up to 6 in. deep. Plants spread with age from vigorous rhizomes. If too rampant, grow in pots or sunken, open-bottom containers to keep under control. |

◁ *Indicates species shown*

Ornamental Grasses for American Gardens

		Height & Spread	Ornamental Features	Hardiness Zones	Growing Conditions
ERAGROSTIS WEEPING LOVE GRASS, AFRICAN LOVE GRASS *Eragrostis curvula*	A group of grasses with tufted forms and small, compressed flowers arrayed in showy clusters. This species has a curving, windswept appearance with 1/16- to 1/8-in.-wide leaves and dark purple flower clusters on arching stems.	Height: 2–4' Spread: 1–3'	Ground cover and soil-binding grass. Delicate flowers in late summer. Fine-textured, semievergreen leaves turn reddish in autumn.	7 to 11	Full sun. Sandy, well-drained soil with ample moisture. Once established, this warm-season perennial grass is quite drought tolerant and adapts to any well-drained site.
ERAGROSTIS PURPLE LOVE GRASS, TUMBLE GRASS *Eragrostis spectabilis*	A clump-forming perennial whose light green, 1/3-in.-wide, 6- to 12-in.-long leaves redden in autumn. The delicate purple clouds of flowers turn tan before the entire cluster breaks off when mature.	Height: 8–30" Spread: 1–1½'	Specimen or massing grass. Wispy flower clusters in midsummer to late summer; use for fresh or dried arrangements. Attractive autumn foliage colors.	6 to 11	Full sun. Sandy, well-drained soil with ample moisture. Once established, this warm-season grass is quite drought tolerant and adapts to any well-drained site.
ERIANTHUS RAVENNA GRASS *Erianthus ravennae*	A coarse, reedlike perennial with white, woolly, plumed flowers. Its gray-green, 1/2-in.-wide, 3- to 4-ft.-long leaves turn bronzy orange to purple in fall. Erianthus is a good substitute for pampas grass (Cortaderia selloana) in cool climates.	Height: 3–12' Spread: 4–5'	Ideal screen, especially at water's edge. Flowers in late summer to early autumn. Use flowers and foliage for fresh or dried arrangements.	5 to 10	Full sun. Moist, well-drained, fertile soil. This species grows best in warm weather. With time the clumps will increase in size. Prune back foliage when tufts start to look ragged.
FESTUCA BLUE-SILVER FESCUE *Festuca cinerea* 'Blausilber'	A low, tufted grass with wiry leaves; short spikes of flowers grow above the clumps of foliage. This species of blue fescue is grown for its striking powder blue leaves.	Height: 4–8" Spread: 6–8"	Ground cover, edging, or rock garden grass. Flowers in spring to early summer.	4 to 9	Full sun to partial shade. Moist, well-drained soil. Blue fescue grows slowly or becomes dormant during hot, dry periods; plant in partial shade and provide supplemental water in hot regions. Cut back the tops in autumn.
FESTUCA MAIRE'S FESCUE *Festuca mairei*	A typical fescue forming dense mounds of fine leaves; the flower clusters rise above the tufts on long stems. The leaves of Maire's fescue are gray green, glossy, 1/8–1/4 in. wide, and remain evergreen.	Height: 2–3' Spread: 1–2'	Massing grass, filler, or ground cover. Evergreen foliage. Flowers in late spring.	5 to 10	Full sun. Moist, well-drained soil. Once established, plants tolerate heat and drought.

			Height & Spread	Ornamental Features	Hardiness Zones	Growing Conditions
	FESTUCA BLUE FESCUE, SHEEP'S FESCUE *Festuca ovina* var. *glauca*	*A low, tufted grass with silvery blue-green, wiry leaves. Short panicles of flowers grow above the clumps of soft foliage. Blue fescue makes an attractive edging plant but does not withstand foot traffic.*	Height: 4–18" Spread: 6–8"	*Edging, ground cover, and rock garden grass. Slender silver-blue leaves. Flowers in spring to early summer.*	4 to 9	*Full sun to partial shade. Prefers moist, well-drained soil but will tolerate some drought if temperatures are not too high. Plant in partial shade and provide supplemental water in hot regions. Cut back tops in autumn.*
	GLYCERIA VARIEGATED MANNA GRASS *Glyceria maxima* 'Variegata'	*Dense, spreading perennial with 2-in.-wide, 4- to 6-in.-long, green leaves streaked with creamy yellow. The leaves emerge pinkish in spring and turn reddish in autumn, before they die back over winter.*	Height: 2–3' Spread: 2–3'	*Ground cover or accent grass, especially for wet soils and water gardens. Variegated foliage with subtle seasonal color changes.*	5 to 10	*Full sun. Wet, humus-rich soil. Plants require constant moisture and will even grow in water up to 6 in. deep. This is a vigorous spreader that should be grown in tubs to keep it in check.*
	HAKONE-CHLOA HAKONE GRASS *Hakonechloa macra* GOLDEN VARIEGATED HAKONECHLOA ◄ *H. macra* 'Aureola'	*A clump-forming perennial that turns reddish pink in autumn. Hakone grass has bright green, 1/3-in.-wide, 3- to 6-in.-long, soft, bamboo-like leaves. 'Aureola' is a golden yellow and green variegated cultivar.*	Height: 6–18" Spread: 1–3'	*Edging or shady ground cover. Foliage offers year-round color interest. Flowers in late summer to early autumn.*	7 to 9	*Partial to full shade. Moist, well-drained, humus-rich soil; does not grow well in clay or where soil dries out completely. This is a slow-growing, cool-season grass that is not invasive.*
	HELICTOTRI-CHON BLUE OAT GRASS *Helictotrichon semper-virens*	*A perennial grass that forms hemispherical clumps of bright blue, stiff evergreen leaves (semievergreen in cold regions). Oatlike, light blue flowers are borne in a 1-sided cluster that fades to yellowish tan as seeds mature.*	Height: 1–5' Spread: 1–1 1/2'	*Perennial border or rock garden grass. Spectacular blue foliage. Attractive flowers in late spring to midsummer; cut for fresh arrangements.*	4 to 8	*Full sun. Well-drained, fertile soil; avoid clay and water-logged soils. This cool-season grass grows best in zones 4–6.*
	HOLCUS VELVET GRASS ◄ *Holcus lanatus* *H. lanatus* var. *variegatus*	*A perennial grass whose velvety stems bear soft, 1/4-in.-wide, 2- to 8-in.-long, gray-green leaves, striped green and white in H. lan. var. variegatus. Light green, fuzzy flowers appear on stalks 1 ft. or more above the semievergreen foliage.*	H. lan. Height: 1–3' Spread: 1–3' Variegatus Height: 4–8" Spread: 8–18"	*Ground cover and meadow grass. Soft foliage. Flowers in mid-spring to mid-summer.*	5 to 9	*Full sun to partial shade. Well-drained, moist, sandy loam. Plants grow best in cool weather; they do poorly when it is hot and humid. With time the tops tend to sprawl and flop over.*

◄ *Indicates species shown*

Ornamental Grasses for American Gardens

			Height & Spread	Ornamental Features	Hardiness Zones	Growing Conditions
	HORDEUM SQUIRRELTAIL GRASS *Hordeum jubatum*	Short-lived perennial grown as an annual. Showy, fox-tail-like, erect or arching flower clusters have dense, stiff bristles, sometimes over 2 in. long, and grow from olive green clumps of 8- to 12-in.-long leaves.	Height: 1–2½' Spread: 1–2'	Filler grass. Showy flowers in summer. Use in fresh arrange-ments; flowers shatter when dried.	4 to 9	Full sun. Moist, well-drained soil. This cool-season grass tolerates heat, wind, and poor soil. Sow seeds directly outdoors in early spring or fall. Plants can become weedy, so cut back after flowering and before fruit matures.
	HYSTRIX BOTTLEBRUSH GRASS *Hystrix patula*	A perennial grass with flower clusters that look like bottlebrushes. The widely spaced flowers have promi-nent bristles pointing away from the stem. The fruits shatter at maturity. The olive green leaves are ⅓ in. wide and 8–12 in. long.	Height: 2–4' Spread: 1–2'	Naturalizing and shady border grass. Attractive flowers in late spring to late summer; cut for fresh arrangements.	5 to 9	Full sun to light shade. Moist, well-drained, preferably sandy soil. This is a cool-season grass that will grow in full sun if sufficient moisture is provided. Avoid hot, dry conditions. Plants will self-sow.
	IMPERATA JAPANESE BLOOD GRASS *Imperata cylindrica* 'Red Baron' (*I. cylindrica* var. *rubra*)	A slow-growing perennial grass with colorful foliage. Slender, upright, 1-ft.-long leaves emerge green with red tips in spring and turn bright blood red, increasing in intensity toward autumn and fading to coppery tan in winter.	Height: 1–1½' Spread: 1½–2'	Border, massing, specimen, and color-accent grass. Brilliant blood red foliage.	5 to 9	Full sun to light shade; partial shade is best. Moist, well-drained soil; avoid heavy, wet, and hot, dry soils. Japanese blood grass grows best in warm weather. Remove stems that revert from red to all-green.
	JUNCUS SOFT RUSH *Juncus effusus* CORKSCREW RUSH *J. effusus* 'Spiralis'	Grasslike, nearly leafless, perennial plants with round, solid stems and greenish brown flowers. Both types have green, ⅛- to ¼-in.-wide tufted stems. 'Spiralis' is smaller and has a twisted form.	*J. effusus* Height: 1–4' Spread: 1–2' 'Spiralis' Height: 1½–2' Spread: 1½–2'	Tufted clumps of foliage for moist soils and water gardens. Flowers in mid- to late spring.	3 to 9	Full sun. Wet, humus-rich soil. Juncus will grow in water up to 6–8 in. deep.
	KOELERIA SILVER HAIR GRASS *Koeleria argentea*	A short-lived, cool-season perennial grass with dense clumps of fine leaves and tall, wandlike flower clus-ters. The ⅛- to ¼-in.-wide, 8- to 10-in.-long leaves are silvery blue-gray. Spikes of white flowers yield tan fruits.	Height: 1–2' Spread: 6–18"	Massing grass or ground cover. Flowers in late spring to early summer.	7 to 9	Full sun. Well-drained soil. Provide moisture when plants are becoming established; thereafter they are quite drought tolerant. Avoid sites that are shady, wet, clayey, or hot and dry.

			Height & Spread	Ornamental Features	Hardiness Zones	Growing Conditions

KOELERIA
JUNE GRASS
Koeleria cristata

A medium-sized grass native to North American prairies. Slender, light green, 1/8-in.-wide leaves grow in tufts. Dense, compact, 6-in., wand-like spikes of tiny flowers taper toward the tip. The seed heads are lustrous.

Height: 1–2'
Spread: 6–8"

Meadow or natural-izing grass. Flowers in late spring. Lustrous, silvery green seed heads.

2 to 8

Full sun to partial shade. Provide well-drained soil that is moist when seedlings or divisions are becoming established; thereafter plants are quite drought tolerant. Do not add fertilizer, as June grass thrives in nutrient-poor soil.

KOELERIA
BLUE HAIR GRASS
Koeleria glauca

A short-lived, cool-season grass forming compact, rounded clumps of silvery blue-gray evergreen leaves, 1/8–1/4 in. wide, 8–10 in. long. Blue-green flowers, held in a cluster 8–12 in. above the foliage, turn brown at maturity.

Height: 6–24"
Spread: 6–12"

Edging or rock garden grass. Flowers in late spring; use in fresh or dried arrangements.

5 to 9

Full sun. Well-drained soil rich in lime. Provide moisture when plants are becoming established; thereafter they are quite drought tolerant. Avoid sites that are shady, wet, clayey, or hot and dry.

KOELERIA
CRESTED HAIR GRASS
Koeleria macrantha

A clump-forming perennial with strong vertical lines. Gray-green to blue-green leaves grow in tufts below the flower spikes. Dense, flattened, glossy green flowers turn golden brown before they shatter from the stem.

Height: 1–1 1/2'
Spread: 6–9"

Ground cover or rock garden grass. Flowers in late spring to early summer.

4 to 9

Full sun to partial shade. Well-drained, alkaline soil. Provide moisture when plants are becoming established; thereafter they are quite drought tolerant. Crested hair grass thrives in nutrient-poor soil; it may become dormant in the heat of summer.

LAGURUS
HARE'S-TAIL GRASS
Lagurus ovatus

An ornamental annual grass with soft, egg-shaped, creamy white, fuzzy fruit heads up to 1 1/2 in. long. The narrow leaves are covered with soft hairs.

Height: 1–2'
Spread: 2–4'

Border or rock garden grass. Flowers in summer. Fruit heads are excellent for dried arrangements.

Hardy annual

Full sun. Average, well-drained soil. Hare's-tail does not compete well with other plants. Start indoors in small peat pots 8 weeks before last frost; plant several seeds in each pot. Transplant in clumps spaced 4 in. apart.

LIRIOPE
BIG BLUE LILYTURF
Liriope muscari

A grasslike member of the lily family with mounds of dark blue-green, 3/4-in.-wide, 2-ft.-long leaves. Spikes of dense hyacinth-like flowers rise above the tufts in summer, followed by pea-sized blue fruits. Variegated cultivars are available.

Height: 8–18"
Spread: 1–2'

Ground cover and massing plant. Evergreen foliage. Attractive lilac-violet flowers in mid-summer, followed by blue fruits.

5 to 10

Full sun to light shade. Evenly moist, well-drained soil. Once established, plants can grow well in dry soil. Cut old leaves back in early spring.

◄ *Indicates species shown*

Ornamental Grasses for American Gardens

			Height & Spread	Ornamental Features	Hardiness Zones	Growing Conditions
	MELICA SIBERIAN MELIC *Melica altissima* SILKY-SPIKE MELIC ◄ *M. ciliata*	Gray-green, clumping perennials with dramatic flower heads that arch and tend to flop over with age. Siberian melic has lacy, lavender flower heads. Silky-spike melic has fluffy, cylindrical clusters of white or yellow flowers.	M. alt. Height: 10–36" Spread: 10–12" M. cili. Height: 10–24" Spread: 10–12"	Border or ground cover grasses. Attractive flowers in mid-spring to late summer.	*M. altissima* 4 to 8 *M. ciliata* 5 to 8	M. altissima, *light shade;* M. ciliata, *full sun to light shade. Moist, well-drained, neutral to slightly alkaline soil; sandy loam is best. Avoid hot, wet sites.*
	MILIUM BOWLES'S GOLDEN GRASS, GOLDEN WOOD MILLET *Milium effusum* 'Aureum'	An evergreen perennial grass that forms loose clumps of light golden green leaves, 1/2 in. wide and 1 ft. long. Golden yellow flowers are held in delicate clusters 1 ft. or so above the foliage.	Height: 6–15" Spread: 6–18"	Naturalizing, woodland, or rock garden grass. Light green foliage. Shimmering golden flowers in mid-spring to early summer.	5 to 9	Light shade. Moist, well-drained, humus-rich soil. This cool-season grass does not grow well where it is hot and dry. Plants spread by runners.
	MISCANTHUS GIANT MISCANTHUS *Miscanthus floridulus* (M. giganteus)	One of the largest species of Miscanthus, a genus of grasses that form large clumps of foliage and have showy, fluffy, plumed flowers on tall canes. The $1^{1}/_{2}$-in.-wide leaves grow up to $2^{1}/_{2}$ ft. long below silvery 1-ft.-long flower clusters.	Height: 8–14' Spread: 5–8'	Specimen, screen, or hedge grass. Bold clumps of foliage turn reddish in autumn. Large, silvery flower clusters in late summer to early autumn; use in fresh or dried arrangements.	5 to 9	Full sun to very light shade. Fertile, moist, well-drained soil. This species grows best in warm weather and tolerates wind and salt spray. Plants are deeply rooted and difficult to remove once established.
	MISCANTHUS AMUR SILVER GRASS, SILVER BANNER GRASS *Miscanthus sacchariflorus*	A spreading grass that looks like a miniature version of sugarcane. Medium green, $^{3}/_{4}$-in.-wide, 8- to 10-in.-long leaves turn orange-brown in autumn. The silvery plumes of feathery flowers persist into winter.	Height: 4–7' Spread: 2–5'	Screen or hedge grass. Bold, upright foliage. White flower clusters in late summer to early autumn; use in fresh or dried arrangements.	5 to 9	Full sun to very light shade. Fertile, moist to wet, well-drained, preferably sandy soil. This species grows best in cool weather. Deeply rooted, it spreads by runners and is difficult to remove once established. It may become a pest in small areas.
	MISCANTHUS MAIDEN GRASS *Miscanthus sinensis* 'Gracillimus' ◄ *M. sinensis* 'Morning Light'	Large grasses with clumps of narrow foliage from which rise 1- to 8-ft. panicles of flowers that remain through winter. 'Gracillimus' has silver midribs and white, fan-shaped flowers. 'Morning Light' has fine, white-edged leaves.	'Gracill.' Height: 5–7' Spread: 2–4' 'M. Light' Height: 4–5' Spread: 2–3'	Background, specimen, or hedge grasses. Erect, delicate clumps of foliage. Plumed flowers in early to late autumn; use in fresh or dried arrangements.	5 to 9	Full sun. Fertile, moist, well-drained soil. M. sinensis grows best when the weather is warm but not hot and humid.

		Height & Spread	Ornamental Features	Hardiness Zones	Growing Conditions
MISCANTHUS SILVER FEATHER GRASS *Miscanthus sinensis* 'Silberfeder'	One of the earliest-flowering Miscanthus cultivars. The silver-white, featherlike plumes of flowers, borne 2–3 ft. above clumps of green foliage, persist into winter. A silver midrib runs the length of each deep green leaf.	Height: 5–6' Spread: 5–6'	Specimen, screen, or hedge grass. Attractive clumps of foliage. White, plumed flower clusters in midsummer to early autumn; use in fresh or dried arrangements.	5 to 9	Full sun. Fertile, moist, well-drained soil. This species grows best when the weather is warm but not hot and humid.
MISCANTHUS PORCUPINE GRASS *Miscanthus sinensis* 'Strictus'	A hardy cultivar with stiff foliage forming narrow, upright clumps. The bright green, 1/2-in.-wide, 8- to 12-in.-long leaves are banded horizontally with yellow and turn tan after autumn frost. The coppery flowers are held 1–2 ft. above the foliage.	Height: 4–6' Spread: 2–3'	Specimen, screen, or hedge grass. Bold, variegated clumps of foliage. Large, plumed flower clusters in late summer to early autumn; use in fresh or dried arrangements.	4 to 9	Full sun. Fertile, moist, well-drained soil. One of the hardier Miscanthus cultivars, porcupine grass also tolerates wet soils.
MISCANTHUS VARIEGATED SILVER GRASS *Miscanthus sinensis* 'Variegatus' ZEBRA GRASS ◄ *M. sinensis* 'Zebrinus'	Variegated cultivars with arching foliage. 'Variegatus' has several creamy white and green stripes running the length of its 1/2-in.-wide leaves. 'Zebrinus' has yellow or white bands across its green leaves.	Height: 4–6' Spread: 3–4'	Specimen or screen grasses. Arched, variegated foliage. 'Variegatus' has pink flowers in late summer; 'Zebrinus' has yellow flowers in early autumn.	5 to 9	M. s. 'Variegatus', full sun to partial shade; 'Zebrinus', full sun. Moist, fertile, well-drained soil. Both cultivars flower best in zones 7–9 and should be given winter protection in zones 5–6.
MISCANTHUS EULALIA *Miscanthus sinensis* var. *condensatus* ◄ *M. s.* var. *condensatus* 'Silberpfeil'	A bold, striking variety of maiden grass that forms upright clumps. The plumes of golden flowers bloom relatively early, turning purplish as they mature in autumn. 'Silberpfeil', sometimes listed as 'Silver Arrow', has white-striped leaves.	Height: 4–5' Spread: 2–3'	Specimen, screen, or hedge grass. Erect clumps of foliage. Attractive flower clusters in midsummer to early autumn; use in fresh or dried arrangements.	4 to 9	Full sun. Fertile, moist, well-drained soil. This is one of the hardiest varieties of maiden grass.
MISCANTHUS FLAME GRASS, PURPLE MAIDEN GRASS *Miscanthus sinensis* var. *purpurescens*	An early-flowering maiden grass with upright clumps of 1/4- to 1/2-in.-wide leaves, medium green in early summer, bright red-orange and purple by late summer, darkening to purple-brown in fall. White flowers rise 1–2 ft. above the foliage.	Height: 3–4' Spread: 2–3'	Specimen, screen, or hedge grass. Upright clumps of foliage with orange to purple autumn color. Flowers in midsummer to early autumn.	6 to 9	Full sun. Fertile, moist, well-drained soil. This is one of the earliest-flowering varieties of maiden grass.

◄ *Indicates species shown*

Ornamental Grasses for American Gardens

			Height & Spread	Ornamental Features	Hardiness Zones	Growing Conditions
	MISCANTHUS EVERGREEN MISCANTHUS *Miscanthus transmorrisonensis*	A handsome grass whose compact clumps of glossy 1/4- to 1/2-in.-wide, 2- to 3-ft.-long leaves remain evergreen where winters are mild. Fluffy, 6- to 8-in.-long plumes of red-brown flowers fade to tan as they mature.	Height: 2–3' Spread: 2–3'	Specimen or low hedge grass. Bold clumps of foliage. Large plumed flower clusters in spring to late summer; use in fresh or dried arrangements.	7 to 10	Full sun to very light shade. Fertile, moist, well-drained soil. Evergreen miscanthus adapts to a wide variety of soils once established and grows best when the weather is warm.
	MOLINIA VARIEGATED MOOR GRASS *Molinia caerulea* 'Variegata'	A group of grasses with showy flowers and clumps of vertical leaves that turn color in autumn. The 1/4- to 1/2-in.-wide, 16-in.-long leaves of variegated moor grass are edged with cream. The purple flowers turn brown as they mature.	Height: 1–3' Spread: 6–12"	Perennial border or specimen grass. Attractive variegated foliage. Delicate flower clusters in late spring to early summer.	4 to 9	Full sun to light shade. Moist, well-drained, acid soil. This is a warm-season grass that grows slowly.
	MOLINIA MOOR GRASS *Molinia caerulea* var. *arundinacea* *M. c.* var. *arundinacea* 'Karl Foerster'	Bold grasses with arching leaves 1/2–3/4 in. wide and 1–1 1/2 ft. long. The flowers are held 3–4 ft. above the foliage, or 6–7 ft. above in 'Karl Foerster'. These plants are beautiful when the flower stalks sway in the breeze.	*M. c. arun.* Height: 2–4' Spread: 1–2' 'Foerster' Height: 2–7' Spread: 1–2'	Perennial border or specimen grass. Erect, arching foliage. Delicate flower clusters in summer.	5 to 9	Full sun to light shade. Moist, well-drained, acid soil. This is a warm-season grass that is slow to establish itself.
	NANDINA HEAVENLY BAMBOO *Nandina domestica*	A member of the barberry family whose textured, evergreen foliage reddens in autumn. The pointed, 1- to 2-in. leaflets resemble bamboo leaves. Flower clusters 6–12 in. long are borne at the branch tips. Shiny red berries follow.	Height: 3–8' Spread: 2–4'	Hedge, screen, or container plant. Bamboolike foliage. White flowers in late spring to early summer. Bright red berries. Autumn leaf color.	7 to 11	Full sun to light shade. Moist, well-drained, acid soil. Once established it is quite drought tolerant. Heavenly bamboo grows slowly.
	OPHIOPOGON DWARF LILYTURF, MONDO GRASS *Ophiopogon japonicus* *O. japonicus* 'Minor'	Members of the lily family, not true grasses, with grasslike evergreen leaves and a sprawling, mounded form. White to pale lilac, 6-petaled flowers are borne in clusters. 'Minor', the smallest cultivar, reaches only 3 in. high.	Height: 3–6" Spread: 4–8"	Creeping, mat-forming ground covers or rock garden plants. Low clumps of evergreen foliage. Small lilac or white flowers in midsummer followed by blue fruits.	7 to 11	Partial to full shade; grows well in shady, moist sites in zones 9–11, but can take more sun in colder regions. Well-drained soil. These lilyturfs can be grown as semi-aquatic plants.

			Height & Spread	Ornamental Features	Hardiness Zones	Growing Conditions
	OPHIOPOGON LILYTURF *Ophiopogon planiscapus* 'Arabicus' ◁ *O. planiscapus* 'Ebony Knight'	*A mat-forming ground cover with $1/4$-in.-wide, 10- to 12-in.-long leaves. The foliage of 'Ebony Knight' is nearly black. 'Arabicus' has purple-black leaves. Spiked clusters of lilac or white flowers produce black berries.*	'Arabicus' Height: 8–10" Spread: 6–12" 'Ebony' Height: 4–6" Spread: 6–12"	*Creeping, clump-forming ground cover. Nearly black foliage. Spikes of small white or lilac flowers in midsummer to late summer. Black fruits.*	6 to 10	*Full sun to light shade. Moist, well-drained soil. Plants spread quickly.*
	ORYZOPSIS INDIAN RICEGRASS *Oryzopsis hymenoides*	*A tufted native perennial of the West whose slender leaves are 6–8 in. long. Twisted, wiry stems bear white-haired flowers whose seeds were once used as food by Native Americans.*	Height: 1–2' Spread: 1–2'	*Meadow, rock garden, or naturalizing grass. Attractive flowers in mid-spring to early summer; use in fresh or dried arrangements.*	3 to 10	*Full sun to light shade. Well-drained, sandy soil. Once established, plants are quite drought tolerant and simply go dormant when weather is excessively hot and dry. To prolong growing season, provide additional moisture.*
	PANICUM SWITCH-GRASS ◁ *Panicum virgatum* *P. virgatum* 'Strictum'	*A versatile bunch-forming grass native to prairies. Erect stems bear 1- to 2-ft.-long green leaves and tall, loose panicles of small reddish flowers. 'Strictum', one of many cultivars, has blue-green leaves and blooms earlier than the species.*	Height: 4–10' Spread: 10–20"	*Ground cover or meadow grass. Narrow, upright clumps of foliage, orange-gold in autumn. Flowers last into winter; cut for fresh arrangements.*	5 to 9	*Full sun. Switch-grass prefers moist, fertile soil, but will grow in a wide variety of conditions. It is very tolerant of wind and salt spray.*
	PENNISETUM FOUNTAIN GRASS ◁ *Pennisetum alopecuroides* *Pennisetum alopecuroides* 'Hameln'	*An attractive fountain grass with arching stems bearing soft, bottlebrush clusters of fuzzy flowers. Its upright clusters of 12- to 20-in.-long leaves become streaked in autumn. The 4- to 5-in. flower plumes are tan or buff to creamy white.*	Height: $1^1/2$–2' Spread: 2–3'	*Specimen, massing, or border grass. Showy, soft, cylindrical flower clusters in midsummer to early autumn. Seed heads last into winter.*	5 to 9	*Full sun to very light shade. Moist soil. This is a slow-growing, warm-season perennial grass that can even be used at water's edge. Divide clumps periodically to encourage vigorous growth and flowering.*
	PENNISETUM BLACK-SEEDED FOUNTAIN GRASS *Pennisetum alopecuroides* var. *viridescens*	*A perennial variety of fountain grass with dark brown to black flowers above lush, arching, dark green to reddish foliage. The 1-ft.-long leaves are $1/2$–$3/4$ in. wide. Sometimes this grass is listed as P. alopecuroides 'Moudry'.*	Height: 1–2' Spread: 15–25"	*Specimen, massing, or border grass. Showy, soft, cylindrical flower clusters in late summer to early autumn. Dark seed heads last into winter.*	5 to 9	*Full sun to light shade. Moist, well-drained soil. This variety can reseed aggressively in moist soil and may become weedy.*

◁ *Indicates species shown*

Ornamental Grasses for American Gardens

		Height & Spread	Ornamental Features	Hardiness Zones	Growing Conditions
PENNISETUM ORIENTAL FOUNTAIN GRASS *Pennisetum orientale*	One of the earliest-blooming fountain grasses. Silky, purple-pink flowers fade to ivory white with maturity. The glossy ¹⁄₈- to ¹⁄₄-in.-wide leaves range in color from gray green to blue green but turn tan by late autumn.	Height: 1–2½' Spread: 12–18"	Specimen, massing, or border grass. Showy, cylindrical, soft flower clusters in late spring to late summer. White seed heads last into winter.	7 to 10	Full sun to light shade. Moist, well-drained, sandy soil; plants benefit from additional moisture. This is a noninvasive warm-season perennial that is somewhat drought tolerant once it is established.
PENNISETUM FOUNTAIN GRASS *Pennisetum setaceum* CRIMSON FOUNTAIN GRASS *Pennisetum setaceum* 'Cupreum'	A fountain grass whose flowering shoots arch over narrow leaves and bear feathery, cylindrical, 9- to 12-in.-long clusters of pinkish flowers. 'Cupreum' has reddish foliage.	Height: 1–2' Spread: 12–15"	Specimen, massing, or border grass. Pink flower clusters in late spring to late summer, and reddish foliage in 'Cupreum'. Seed heads last into winter.	8 to 11	Full sun. Well-drained soil. Crimson fountain grass thrives on neglect but is sensitive to frost. It tends to become weedy in warm, dry regions, spreading by seeds. It can be grown as an annual in zones 5–8.
PENNISETUM FEATHERTOP *Pennisetum villosum*	A frost-sensitive fountain grass that forms a creeping mat of soft green leaves and stems covered with downy hairs. Creamy white to light green 3- to 4-in. flower clusters arch above the foliage and turn tan with age.	Height: 1–2' Spread: 1–2'	Ground cover or massing grass. Soft foliage and flower clusters. Attractive flowers in late summer to early autumn; excellent for dried or fresh arrangements.	9 to 11	Full sun to light shade. Moist, well-drained, fertile soil. P. villosum grows as a perennial in zones 9–11, as an annual elsewhere (sow seeds in late spring). It has become weedy in the Southwest, self-seeding aggressively.
PHALARIS REED CANARY GRASS *Phalaris arundinacea* RIBBON GRASS *P. arundinacea* var. *picta*	Perennial grasses whose spreading shoots and towering 7-in. spikes of soft white or pink flowers add drama to garden borders. The broad (³⁄₄- to 1-in.-wide), flat leaves are uniform green. P. a. var. picta has white-edged leaves.	Height: 2–5' Spread: 6–12"	Specimen or low hedge grass. Flowers in late spring to early summer. Use flowers and foliage in dried or fresh arrangements.	4 to 9	Partial sun to partial shade; plants prefer afternoon shade in warm climates. Moist soil; these plants will even grow in waterlogged soil and in several inches of standing water.
PHALARIS BIRDSEED GRASS, CANARY GRASS *Phalaris canariensis*	An annual grass that is a source of commercial birdseed, hence its common name. The ¹⁄₂-in.-wide, 9-in.-long leaves grow in tufts. Variegated flowers are clustered on oval spikes that turn a shiny yellow as they mature.	Height: 1–3' Spread: 1–2'	Border or rock garden grass. Shiny yellow flowers in egg-shaped clusters in late spring to midsummer.	Hardy annual	Full sun. Moist, well-drained soil. Sow seeds directly outdoors in early spring. Canary grass may become weedy.

			Height & Spread	Ornamental Features	Hardiness Zones	Growing Conditions
	PHORMIUM NEW ZEALAND FLAX *Phormium tenax* ◀ *Phormium tenax* 'Variegatum'	A large perennial of the agave family for warm-climate gardens with plenty of space. Striking sword-shaped, 5-in.-wide leaves with red-orange lines on their edges grow to 9 ft. long. Dull red flowers grow in clusters above the foliage.	Height: 8–15' Spread: 5–10'	Bold specimen plant. Striking foliage. Red flowers in summer. 'Variegatum' has leaves with creamy yellow and white stripes.	9 to 10	Full sun to light shade. Well-drained soil. This fast-growing plant is not at all fussy and can withstand periodically wet soils or drought. However, it is prone to root rot if soil is wet for prolonged periods.
	PHYLLO-STACHYS YELLOW-GROOVE BAMBOO *Phyllostachys aureosulcata*	One of the hardiest bamboos. The 1½-in.-wide canes are flattened on one side and turn from medium green to olive green with yellow grooves as they mature. Dark green leaves are 4–6 in. long. Young shoots are edible.	Height: 15–30' Spread: 10–15'	Screen or hedge plant. Attractive deep green leaves. Canes have yellow grooves.	6 to 11	Full sun to light shade. Fertile, moist, well-drained soil. Protect plants from wind. This bamboo can become aggressive in warm regions, spreading by runners. Plant it in bottomless tubs to prevent spreading.
	PHYLLO-STACHYS BLACK BAMBOO *Phyllostachys nigra*	A bamboo whose 1½-in.-wide stems are green the first year but turn black at the joints and white below the joints the second year. The very thin leaves are 2–5 in. long. Cultivars with black-speckled shoots in the second year are available.	Height: 10–26' Spread: 10–15'	Screen or hedge plant. Attractive thin green leaves. Canes have black joints.	7 to 11	Full sun to light shade. Moist, well-drained soil. In regions with hot summers, plant black bamboo where afternoon shade is available. Plants spread by runners.
	RHYNCHELY-TRUM CHAMPAGNE GRASS, NATAL GRASS, RUBY GRASS *Rhynchelytrum repens*	A short-lived, frost-sensitive perennial with tufts of flat, green, ¼-in.-wide, 8- to 12-in.-long leaves that come to a sharp point. Silky, pink flowers are borne in loose clusters, 3–6 in. long and 2–3 in. wide.	Height: 3–6' Spread: 2–3'	Border or specimen grass. Pink flowers in late summer through fall.	9 to 11	Full sun to light shade. Well-drained, sandy soil. In cooler regions, grow natal grass as an annual; start seeds indoors in early spring and transplant outdoors after all danger of frost has passed.
	SASA KUMA BAMBOO GRASS *Sasa veitchii*	A bamboo with thin (¼-in.) canes that are waxy lavender at the joints. The 1- to 2-in.-wide, 5- to 8-in.-long leaves are dark green above and pale green below. The edges of the leaves turn light tan in autumn.	Height: 2–3' Spread: 2–3'	Low screen or hedge grass. Attractive thin stems with purplish joints.	7 to 11	Light shade. Moist, well-drained soil. This species can spread rampantly by runners; plant with root barriers to curb its aggressiveness.

◀ *Indicates species shown*

Ornamental Grasses for American Gardens

			Height & Spread	Ornamental Features	Hardiness Zones	Growing Conditions
	SCHIZACHY-RIUM LITTLE BLUESTEM *Schizachyrium scoparium*	A native perennial grass at its most beautiful in fall, when its tufts of thin, ¼-in.-wide, blue-green leaves turn wine red and its thin, 2- to 3-in.-long clusters of fuzzy flowers glisten white in the sun. The foliage is a lovely tan-orange through winter.	Height: 2–5' Spread: 6–12"	Meadow or border grass. Bright white, hairy flowers in late summer to early autumn. Rusty red to wine red autumn foliage.	3 to 10	Full sun. Moist, well-drained soil. This slow-growing, warm-season grass forms clumps in dry soil; its growth is more spreading and sodlike in moist soil.
	SCIRPUS BULRUSH *Scirpus cernuus* BANDED BULRUSH ◀ *S. tabernaemontani* var. *zebrinus*	Tussock-forming, grasslike perennials related to sedges. S. cernuus has arching 9-in.-long, green leaves and small whitish flowers. The leaves of S. t. var. zebrinus have horizontal cream-colored bands alternating with green and are more upright.	S. cern. Height: 6–12" Spread: 1–2' S. t. zeb. Height: 2–4' Spread: 2–4'	Water garden and wetland plants. Arching stems. Flowers in late spring to midsummer.	S. cern. 9 to 10 S. t. zeb. 7 to 9	Full sun to light shade. Constantly moist or wet, humus-rich soil. Both types can be grown in standing water several inches deep.
	SESLERIA AUTUMN MOOR GRASS ◀ *Sesleria autumnalis* BLUE MOOR GRASS *S. caerulea*	Handsome grasses with clumps of thin evergreen leaves. S. autumnalis has silver flowers and bright yellow-green leaves; S. caerulea has twisted blue-green leaves and narrow spikes of purple flowers that turn tan at maturity.	Height: 6–18" Spread: 6–18"	Ground cover grasses. Attractive foliage. S. autumnalis flowers in autumn, S. caerulea in spring.	5 to 9	Full sun to light shade. Moist, well-drained, humus-rich, alkaline soil. These are cool-season grasses.
	SETARIA PALM GRASS *Setaria palmifolia*	A bold, evergreen plant whose pleated, palmlike leaves form upright, arching clumps. The leaves are 2–3 in. wide and 1–3 ft. long. The 16-in.-long panicles of fuzzy flowers arch above the foliage.	Height: 3–6' Spread: 3–6'	Specimen or screen grass. Interesting leaves. Flowers in early summer to late summer; cut for fresh and dried arrangements.	9 to 10	Full sun to light shade. Moist, well-drained, fertile soil; adapts to clayey and sandy soils. Palm grass tends to be weedy in warm climates. It can be grown north of zone 9 if dug up in autumn and stored at temperatures above freezing over winter.
	SISYRINCHIUM BLUE-EYED GRASS *Sisyrinchium angustifolium*	A native of the iris family with grasslike leaves. Narrow stems support clusters of ½-in. blue flowers with yellow centers. After flowers wither, the plant blends into the grassy landscape.	Height: 5–20" Spread: 6–12"	Meadow or border plant. Clear blue flowers for short period in spring.	3 to 8	Full sun to partial shade. Average garden or meadow soil. Blue-eyed grass is not particular about growing conditions.

			Height & Spread	Ornamental Features	Hardiness Zones	Growing Conditions
	SORGHAS-TRUM INDIAN GRASS, WOOD GRASS *Sorghastrum avenaceum* *(S. nutans)*	A perennial bunchgrass, native to the prairies, with ¼- to ½-in.-wide, 8- to 12-in.-long leaves. Feathery, golden bronze flowers have short, twisted bristles, giving the clusters an airy appearance. The plant turns yellow-orange in autumn.	Height: 2–5' Spread: 1–3'	Meadow or border grass. Flowers in late summer to early autumn. Glossy seed heads and orange foliage in autumn.	4 to 9	Full sun to light shade. Moist, well-drained soil. This robust, warm-season grass is drought tolerant once it is established.
	SPARTINA PRAIRIE CORDGRASS, SLOUGH GRASS *Spartina pectinata* ◄ *S. pectinata* 'Aureomarginata'	A tall perennial grass, native to wet prairies, with stiff branches and 2½-ft.-long, rough-edged leaves. The brown flowers are clustered in 1-sided combs. 'Aureomarginata' has yellow stripes running along the edges of its leaves.	Height: 2–7' Spread: 2–5'	Wet meadows and water gardens. Stems have arching form. Flowers in mid-summer; cut for fresh or dried arrangements. Golden yellow autumn foliage.	4 to 9	Full sun to light shade. Moist or wet, fertile soil; will tolerate wet, clayey soils. This is a warm-season grass that can grow aggressively.
	SPODIO-POGON FROST GRASS, SILVERSPIKE GRASS *Spodiopogon sibiricus*	A grass whose fuzzy, stiff, bamboolike leaves (1 in. wide and 6–8 in. long) form upright clumps. Foliage is light green in summer and develops purple-red tones in autumn. Conical clusters of purple flowers persist into winter.	Height: 4–5' Spread: 2–3'	Specimen, border, or naturalizing grass. Flowers in mid-summer to early autumn. Autumn leaf color. Flowers last into winter; use for dried or fresh arrangements.	5 to 9	Full sun to light shade. Moist, well-drained, fertile, humus-rich soil. Silverspike grass grows best where the climate is cool and moist; provide shade where summers tend to be hot.
	SPOROBOLUS NORTHERN DROPSEED *Sporobolus heterolepis*	Perennial native prairie grass that forms dense, lush tufts. These attractive clumps turn golden as fall approaches. Light green, arching leaves are ⅛ in. wide and several feet long. Showy flowers are borne in loose, 8-in.-long clusters.	Height: 1½–5' Spread: 1–1½'	Meadow and border grass. Attractive flowers in mid- to late summer. Fine-textured, bright green foliage turns yellow in autumn.	3 to 9	Full sun. Northern dropseed prefers well-drained soil that is dry and rocky, but grows well in a wide range of soil conditions as long as drainage is good. Once established, this cool-season grass is quite tolerant of heat and drought.
	STENOTAPH-RUM STRIPED ST. AUGUS-TINE GRASS *Stenotaphrum secundatum* 'Variegatum'	A low, spreading, variegated cream and light green perennial grass that can be grown as a ground cover or lawn substitute. Glossy, ¼- to ½-in.-wide, 2- to 4-in.-long leaves trail on the ground. Plants remain evergreen where winters are warm.	Height: 4–6' Spread: 1–10'	Ground cover, lawn, or rock wall grass. Cream-and-green-striped leaves. White or pale green flowers in late summer.	9 to 11	Full sun. Moist, well-drained soil. This grass tolerates sandy and clayey soils, wind, and salt spray as long as enough moisture is provided. It is, however, very sensitive to frost.

◄ *Indicates species shown*

Ornamental Grasses for American Gardens

			Height & Spread	Ornamental Features	Hardiness Zones	Growing Conditions
STIPA NEEDLEGRASS ◀ *Stipa calamagrostis* NEEDLE-AND-THREAD *S. comata*		Perennial grasses named for the prominent curly hairs and long bristles on their fruit heads. S. calamagrostis has thin, rolled, bluish evergreen leaves. S. comata has narrow, 6- to 12-in.-long leaves and slender, twisted bristles.	S. calam. Height: 2–3' Spread: 1–2' S. comata Height: 1–2' Spread: 6–12"	Meadow or border grasses. Flowers in late spring to midsummer. Fruit heads are stunning when backlit by the sun.	S. calam. 6 to 11 S. comata 3 to 9	Full sun to light shade. Moist, well-drained, preferably sandy soil. Avoid poorly drained sites.
STIPA GIANT FEATHER GRASS ◀ *Stipa gigantea* PORCUPINE GRASS *S. spartea*		Densely tufted perennial grasses. S. gigantea forms a mound of gray-green, arching leaves from which 1½-ft. panicles of yellow flowers emerge. S. spartea bears clusters of nodding flowers with long, stiff bristles on 3-ft. stems.	S. gigan. Height: 1½–7' Spread: 2–3' S. spartea Height: 2–3' Spread: 1–2'	Specimen or meadow grasses. Open clusters of dangling flowers in midsummer.	S. gigan. 7 to 9 S. spartea 3 to 8	Full sun to light shade. Evenly moist, fertile, well-drained soil. These cool-season grasses do not grow well in wet, clayey soil.
TRITICUM WHEAT ◀ *Triticum aestivum* POULARD WHEAT *T. turgidum*		Annual grasses with fat, round flower spikes clustered in 2 rows. Often the flowers bear long bristles that give the fruit heads ornamental value. Poulard wheat includes durum and other gluten-rich types.	Height: 1½–4' Spread: 6–8"	Border and agricultural grasses. Flowers in spring to summer, depending on cultivar. Attractive fruit heads with or without long bristles.	Hardy annual	Full sun. Moist, well-drained soil. Sow winter wheat in autumn to harvest the following spring. Sow spring wheat in early spring to harvest in autumn.
TYPHA NARROW-LEAVED CATTAIL ◀ *Typha angustifolia* *T. angustifolia* 'Variegata'		Perennial plants with 3- to 6-ft.-long slender leaves forming erect clumps. Stout stems rise above leaves and bear yellow male flowers on top of the densely clustered brown female blooms that form the cattail. 'Variegata' has striped leaves.	Height: 3–5' Spread: 1–2'	Wetland plant for moist soil. Slender foliage in erect clumps. Flowers in early summer. Fuzzy, brown seed heads persist into late autumn.	5 to 9	Full sun to partial shade. Moist or wet, humus-rich soil. Cattails can grow in standing water up to 1 ft. deep. They usually are not overly aggressive, but spreading can be stopped with root barriers.
TYPHA COMMON CATTAIL *Typha latifolia*		Perennial plants forming erect clumps of swordlike, 1- to 1½-in.-wide leaves that grow to 6 ft. high. Male flowers are carried on straight stems above dark brown female flowers. Fuzzy, brown seed heads are produced by female flowers.	Height: 4–8' Spread: 1–2'	Wetland plant for bog gardens, water gardens, or moist to wet soil. Heavier looking than T. angustifolia. Fuzzy brown elongated seed heads to 6 in. last long into autumn.	3 to 10	Full sun or light shade. Moist or wet, humus-rich soil. Common cattail can grow in standing water up to 1 ft. deep. It spreads aggressively by rhizomes if not contained.

			Height & Spread	Ornamental Features	Hardiness Zones	Growing Conditions
	UNIOLA SEA OATS, SPIKE-GRASS *Uniola paniculata*	A native dune-building grass of the Southeast, protected by state laws. Clump-forming, light green leaves are $1/4$–$1/2$ in. wide and 2–3 ft. long. Very attractive flattened, drooping, light green flower clusters turn tan as fruits mature.	Height: 3–8' Spread: 2–4'	Dune plant for sandy coastal gardens. Flowers in mid-summer. Very attractive flower and seed clusters; cut for dried or fresh arrangements.	7 to 10	Full sun. Well-drained, sandy soil with even moisture below the soil surface. An ideal dune plant for coastal areas south of the Carolinas, sea oats need frequent sand deposition to continue to grow. This grass is sensitive to foot traffic.
	VETIVERIA VETIVER, KHUS-KHUS *Vetiveria zizanioides*	A clump-forming perennial whose aromatic roots are used to make baskets and potpourri. The bold, 3- to 5-ft. leaves bend at an angle about 1 ft. from their tips, forming a dramatic clump. Fluffy, 1-ft. flower plumes rise above the leaves.	Height: 4–8' Spread: 2–4'	Specimen, screen, or hedge grass. Erect clump of foliage is distinctively bent. Attractive flower clusters in late summer to early autumn; use in fresh or dried arrangements.	9 to 11	Full sun to light shade. Moist, humus-rich, well-drained soil. Once established, this warm-season grass tolerates drought and adapts to many types of soil.
	XANTHOR-RHOEA GRASS TREE ◀ *Xanthorrhoea arborea* *X. quadrangulata*	A tender tropical perennial of the lily family that produces a short, thick trunk topped by masses of dark green, leathery, grasslike leaves. The leaves of X. arborea are flat; those of X. quadrangulata are square in cross section.	X. arb. Height: 2–4' Spread: 4–10' X. quad. Height: 2–10' Spread: 4–10'	Specimen plants. Large mounds of long, grasslike leaves. Flowers in summer.	10 to 11	Full sun to light shade. Moist, well-drained, humus-rich soil. These slow-growing plants are drought resistant once established.
	XEROPHYLLUM MOUNTAIN ASPHODEL, TURKEYBEARD *Xerophyllum asphode-loides*	A member of the lily family native to pine barrens in the East. Narrow ($1/10$ in.), wiry, grasslike leaves form clumps from which emerge shoots bearing 3- to 6-in., domed clusters of fragrant, $1/4$-in., white flowers.	Height: 1–5' Spread: 2–3'	Rock garden, border, or naturalizing plant. Mounded light green foliage. Showy clusters of fragrant white flowers in summer.	5 to 8	Full sun to light shade. Moist, well-drained, humus-rich, acid soil.
	ZIZANIA ANNUAL WILD RICE, INDIAN RICE *Zizania aquatica*	An annual grass grown for its gourmet seeds. The $3/4$- to $1 1/2$-in.-wide leaves grow on tall shoots. Flower clusters are 1–2 ft. long, with female flowers at the top and male flowers dangling below.	Height: 6–10' Spread: 2–3'	Bold grass for water gardens. Large clusters of flowers in summer. Gather ripe fruit before it shatters off the stems.	Hardy annual	Full sun to light shade. Moist to wet soil; can grow in standing water up to 9 in. deep. Wild rice seeds require damp storage during the winter to germinate well. Sow seeds outdoors in early spring.

◀ *Indicates species shown*

Ornamental Grasses for Different Uses

Ornamental grasses serve many purposes in the garden. This list will help you decide which grasses best suit your gardening needs. If your primary interest is grass color, for example, look under Colored and Variegated Leaves. Here you will find a list of grasses by Latin names with the characteristic colors and patterns of the leaves in parentheses. Or you may wish to use ornamental grasses as specimen plants, screens, or ground covers, or place them in shady areas. Check the appropriate lists for grasses that fall under these categories. Also, don't forget that the main text includes examples of grasses for rock gardens (page 21), meadows and prairies (page 26), or wet areas (page 75), as well as grasses that are drought tolerant (page 72), or good for cutting and drying (pages 46–47). For more information on the grasses listed here or in the main text, check the plant encyclopedia (beginning on page 102).

Colored and Variegated Leaves

Alopecurus pratensis 'Aureus' (golden yellow)

Arrhenatherum elatius var. *bulbosum* 'Variegatum' (white and green striped)

Arundinaria pygmaea 'Variegatus' (white stripes)

Arundo donax var. *variegata* (white stripes)

Carex comans 'Bronze Form' (bronzy tan)

C. comans 'Frosty Curls' (white tips)

C. conica 'Variegata' (white edges)

C. morrowii 'Aureovariegata' (yellow stripes)

C. stricta 'Bowles's Golden' (yellow)

Dactylis glomerata 'Variegata' (silver and green stripes)

Elymus condensatus 'Canyon Prince' (blue)

E. glaucus (blue-green)

Festuca cinerea 'Blausilber' (powder blue)

F. ovina var. *glauca* (silvery blue-green)

Glyceria maxima 'Variegata' (yellow streaks)

Hakonechloa macra 'Aureola' (variegated with yellow and green)

Helictotrichon sempervirens (blue)

Holcus lanatus var. *variegatus* (white and green stripes)

Imperata cylindrica 'Red Baron' (red)

Koeleria argentea (silvery blue-gray)

K. glauca (silvery blue-gray)

Milium effusum 'Aureum' (golden green)

Miscanthus sinensis 'Morning Light' (white edges)

M. sinensis 'Strictus' (horizontal yellow bands)

M. sinensis 'Variegatus' (white and green stripes)

M. sinensis 'Zebrinus' (horizontal yellow or white bands)

M. sinensis var. *condensatus* 'Silberpfeil' (white stripes)

Molinia caerulea 'Variegata' (cream edges)

Ophiopogon planiscapus 'Ebony Knight' (black)

Panicum virgatum 'Strictum' (blue-green)

Phalaris arundinacea var. *picta* (white edges)

Schizachyrium scoparium (blue-green)

Scirpus tabernaemontani var. *zebrinus* (horizontal cream bands)

Sesleria autumnalis (yellow-green)

S. caerulea (blue-green)

Spartina pectinata 'Aureomarginata' (yellow stripes at edges)

Stenotaphrum secundatum 'Variegatum' (variegated with cream)

Typha angustifolia 'Variegata' (white stripes)

Specimen Plants

Arundo donax

Calamagrostis spp.

Carex pendula

Coix lacryma-jobi

Cordyline australis

Cortaderia spp.

Eragrostis spectabilis

Miscanthus spp.

Molinia spp.

Pennisetum spp.

Phalaris spp.

Phormium tenax

Rhynchelytrum repens

Setaria palmifolia

Spodiopogon sibiricus

Stipa gigantea

Vetiveria zizanioides

Xanthorrhoea spp.

For Screening

Arundo donax

Bambusa spp.

Calamagrostis acutiflora var. *stricta*

Cortaderia spp.

Erianthus ravennae

Miscanthus spp.

Nandina domestica

Phyllostachys spp.

Sasa veitchii

Setaria palmifolia

Vetiveria zizanioides

For Ground Cover

Arundinaria pygmaea

Briza media

Buchloe dactyloides

Carex conica 'Variegata'

C. morrowii cvs.

C. muskingumensis

C. testacea

C. texensis

C. tumulicola

Elymus spp.

Equisetum hyemale

Eragrostis curvula

Festuca spp.

Glyceria maxima 'Variegata'

Hakonechloa macra

Holcus lanatus

Koeleria argentea

K. macrantha

Liriope muscari

Melica spp.

Ophiopogon spp.

Panicum virgatum

Pennisetum villosum

Sesleria spp.

Stenotaphrum secundatum 'Variegatum'

For Shade

Acorus spp.

Alopecurus pratensis 'Aureus'

Anthoxanthum odoratum

Arrhenatherum elatius var. *bulbosum* 'Variegatum'

Arundinaria pygmaea

Bambusa spp.

Calamagrostis arundinacea 'Karl Foerster'

Carex spp.

Chasmanthium latifolium

Cymbopogon citratus

Cyperus spp.

Dactylis glomerata 'Variegata'

Deschampsia caespitosa

Elymus canadensis

E. condensatus

E. glaucus

Equisetum hyemale

Festuca cinerea 'Blausilber'

F. ovina var. *glauca*

Hakonechloa macra

Holcus lanatus

Hystrix patula

Imperata cylindrica 'Red Baron'

Koeleria cristata

K. macrantha

Liriope muscari

Melica spp.

Milium effusum 'Aureum'

Miscanthus sinensis 'Variegatus'

Molinia spp.

Nandina dmoestica

Ophiopogon spp.

Oryzopsis hymenoides

Pennisetum alopecuroides var. *viridescens*

P. orientale

P. villosum

Phalaris arundinacea

Phormium tenax

Phyllostachys spp.

Rhynchelytrum repens

Sasa veitchii

Scirpus spp.

Sesleria spp.

Setaria palmifolia

Sisyrinchium angustifolium

Sorghastrum avenaceum

Spartina pectinata

Spodiopogon sibiricus

Stipa spp.

Typha spp.

Vetiveria zizanioides

Xanthorrhoea spp.

Xerophyllum asphodeloides

Zizania aquatica

Plant Hardiness Zone Map

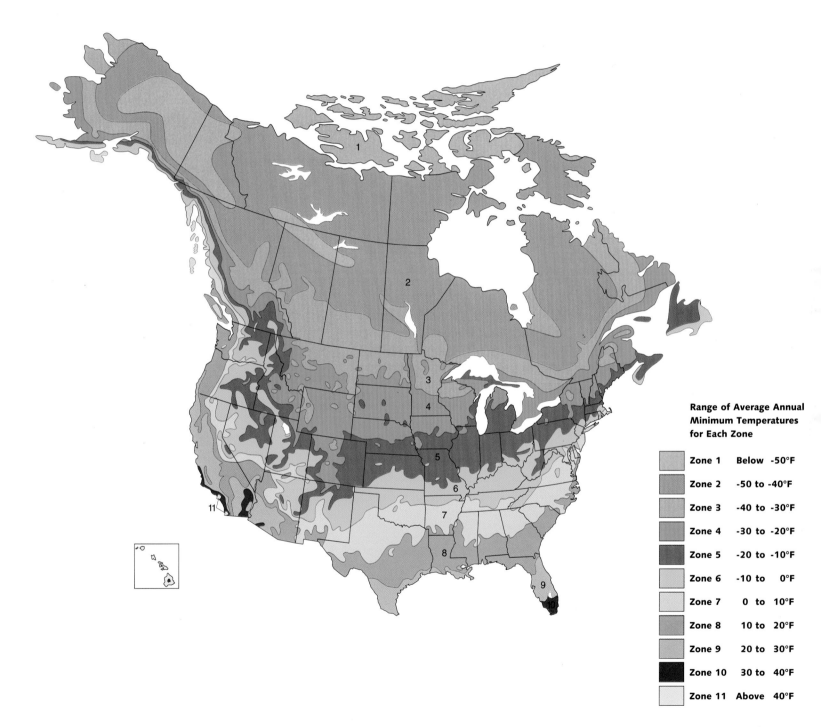

Range of Average Annual Minimum Temperatures for Each Zone

	Zone 1	Below -50°F
	Zone 2	-50 to -40°F
	Zone 3	-40 to -30°F
	Zone 4	-30 to -20°F
	Zone 5	-20 to -10°F
	Zone 6	-10 to 0°F
	Zone 7	0 to 10°F
	Zone 8	10 to 20°F
	Zone 9	20 to 30°F
	Zone 10	30 to 40°F
	Zone 11	Above 40°F

Resources for Ornamental Grasses

There are many dependable mail-order suppliers that can be helpful for landscaping with ornamental grasses. A selection is included here. Most have catalogues available upon request (some charge a fee). An excellent source of further resources is Gardening by Mail *by Barbara J. Barton. Updates on each edition are provided three times a year, available through subscription (forms provided in back of book); a new edition comes out every few years. To obtain this book check your local bookstore or contact the publisher: Houghton Mifflin Co., 222 Berkeley Street, Boston, MA 02116. Telephone: (617) 351-5000.*

Plants and Seeds

Kurt Bluemel, Inc.
2740 Greene Lane
Baldwin, MD 21013
410-557-7229
Specializes in ornamental grasses, sedges, and rushes; also bamboos, ferns, and aquatic plants.

Bluestone Perennials
7211 Middle Ridge Road
Madison, OH 44057
800-852-5243
Sells perennials and selected shrubs, ornamental grasses, and ferns.

Carroll Gardens, Inc.
Box 310
444 East Main Street
Westminster, MD 21158
410-848-5422
Complete catalogue of perennials, including ornamental grasses.

Coastal Gardens & Nursery
4611 Socastee Blvd.
Myrtle Beach, SC 29575
803-293-2000
Catalogue includes many ornamental grasses.

DeGiorgi Seeds & Goods
6011 'N' Street
Omaha, NE 68117-1634
800-858-2580
Plants and seeds of a wide variety of grasses.

Double D Nursery
2215 Dogwood Lane
Arnoldsville, GA 30619
800-438-7685
Nursery products featuring ground covers, perennials, grasses, and herbs.

Garden Place
6780 Heisley Road
P.O. Box 388
Mentor, OH 44061-0388
216-255-3705
Nursery-grown plants; all grasses grown from division.

Greenlee Nursery
301 E. Franklin Avenue
Pomona, CA 91766
909-629-9045
Ornamental grasses, sedges, and rushes.

Holbrook Farm & Nursery
P.O. Box 368
115 Lance Road
Fletcher, NC 28732
704-891-7790
Specializes in perennials, wildflowers, grasses, and selected trees and shrubs.

Klehm Nursery
Route 5, Box 197
Penny Road
South Barrington, IL 60010-9389
800-553-3715
Peonies and other perennials; a selection of grasses.

Lake County Nursery, Inc.
P.O. Box 122
Perry, OH 44081-0122
216-259-5571
Ornamental grasses, ferns, and ground covers.

Limerock Ornamental Grasses
Route 1, Box 111-C
Port Matilda, PA 16870
814-692-2272
Specializes in grasses and native plants.

Mellinger's
2310 W. South Range Road
North Lima, OH 44452-9731
216-549-9861
Seeds and plants for selected grasses.

Milaeger's Gardens
4838 Douglas Avenue
Racine, WI 53402-2498
800-669-9956
Over 300 varieties of perennials, including grasses and vines.

J.E. Miller Nurseries, Inc.
5060 West Lake Road
Canandaigua, NY 14424
800-836-9630
Catalogue includes a selection of ornamental grasses.

Park Seed Co.
Cokesbury Road
Greenwood, SC 29647
800-223-7333
Catalogue offers seeds, plants, bulbs, tools; small selection of grasses.

Shady Oaks Nursery
112 Tenth Ave. SE
Waseca, MN 56093
507-835-5033
Good selection of plants for shade, including ferns and some grasses.

Spring Hill Nurseries
6523 N. Galena Road
Peoria, IL 61632
800-582-8527
Plants and bulbs, especially perennials, shrubs, ground covers, and roses.

Stokes Seeds, Inc.
Box 548
Buffalo, NY 14240-0548
716-695-6980
Flower and vegetable seeds and supplies for commercial farmers and home gardeners.

Thompson & Morgan
P.O. Box 1308
Jackson, NJ 08527
800-367-7333
Seeds for perennial and annual grasses.

K. Van Bourgondien &
Sons, Inc.
245 Farmingdale Road
P.O. Box 1000
Babylon, NY 11702-0598
800-552-9996
Although the Van
Bourgondien name is
equated with bulbs, the
perennial catalogue
includes many ornamental
grasses.

André Viette Farm &
Nursery
Route 1, Box 16
Fishersville, VA 22939
703-943-2315
Nursery-grown perennial
grasses.

Wayside Gardens
1 Garden Lane
Hodges, SC 29695
800-845-1124
Sophisticated ornamental
plants, including many
hard-to-find perennials.

White Flower Farm
Route 63
Litchfield, CT 06759
203-496-9624
Shrubs, perennials, sup-
plies, books, and gifts.
Particularly beautiful color
catalogue.

Native Grass Specialties

Abundant Life Seed
Foundation
P.O. Box 772
Port Townsend,
WA 98368
206-385-5660
Seeds of many flowers,
grains, wildflowers, trees,
and shrubs.

Boothe Hill Wildflowers
23B Boothe Hill
Chapel Hill, NC 27514
919-967-4091
Native grasses and wild-
flowers.

Ernst Crownvetch Farms
RD 5
Meadville, PA 16335
800-873-3321
Grass seed and live plants;
emphasis on conservation
plantings.

Lofts Seed, Inc.
P.O. Box 146
Bound Brook, NJ 08805
908-356-8700
Seeds of native and orna-
mental grasses, wildflow-
ers, and mixes.

The Natural Garden
38W443 Highway 64
St. Charles, IL 60175
708-584-0150
Native plants, including
many prairie grasses.

Plants of the Wild
Box 866
Tekoa, WA 99033
509-284-2848
Native grasses, plants, and
wildflowers.

Prairie Ridge Nursery
9738 Overland Road
Mount Horeb, WI 53572
608-437-5245
Seeds and plants of native
grasses, sedges, and wildflowers.

Redwood City Seed Co.
P.O. Box 361
Redwood City, CA 94064
415-325-7333
Native grass seeds and
plants, as well as books
and information on native
revegetation.

Stock Seed Farms, Inc.
28008 Mill Road
Murdock, NE 68407
402-867-3771
Native grass seed; wild-
flowers.

Regional Specialties

High Altitude Gardens
P.O. Box 4619
Ketchum, ID 83340
800-874-7333
Choice selection of native
grasses with helpful growing condition chart in
catalogue.

Larner Seeds
P.O. Box 407
Bolinas, CA 94924
415-868-9407
Wildlflowers, grasses, trees,
and shrubs; specializes in
California plant seeds.

Missouri Wildflowers
Nursery
9814 Pleasant Hill Road
Jefferson City, MO 65109
314-496-3492
Native grasses and plants
of Missouri and the
Midwest.

Native American Seed
3400 Long Prairie
Flower Mound,
TX 75028
214-539-0534
Native wildflowers and
grasses of Texas and
Oklahoma region.

Native Gardens
5737 Fisher Lane
Greenback, TN 37742
615-856-0220
Nursery-propagated native
grasses for the Southeast.

Niche Gardens
1111 Dawson Road
Chapel Hill, NC 27516
919-967-0078
Nursery-propagated
native plants; selected
ornamental grasses; special
emphasis on southeastern
U.S. native species.

Plants of the Southwest
Agua Fria Route 6
Box 11-A
Santa Fe, NM 87501
800-788-7333
Catalogue includes native
grasses of the southwest-
ern U.S.

Prairie Moon Nursery
Route 3, Box 163
Winona, MN 55987
507-452-1362
Plants and seeds of grasses
and wildflowers native to
the upper Midwest.

Prairie Nursery
P.O. Box 306
Westfield, WI 53964
608-296-3679
Plants and seeds for native
prairieland species.

Prairie Seed Source
P.O. Box 83
North Lake, WI 53064
No phone orders.
Catalogue features prairie
plants, including wildflow-
ers and grasses.

Index

Photo Credits

All photography credited as
follows is copyright © 1995 by
the individual photographers.
Karen Bussolini: pp. 22, 30
(Helictotrichon sempervirens),
36 (center), 39, 41, 66, 74;
David Cavagnaro: pp. 30
*(Miscanthus sinensis, Festuca
californica* 'Serpentine Blue'*)*,
33 (right), 37, 40, 43; **Walter
Chandoha:** pp. 49, 82, 91;
Christine M. Douglas: pp. 83,
97; **Derek Fell:** pp. 13 (left and
right), 25, 27 (bottom), 93;
Mick Hales: pp. 4, 10, 42, 46,
56–57, 78; **Saxon Holt:** pp. 23,
30 *(Hakonechloa macra*
'Aureola'*)*, 34, 36 (right), 44
(center and right), 45 *(Miscanthus sinensis* 'Gracillimus'*)*,
51 (bottom); **Dency Kane:** pp.
30 *(Miscanthus sinensis* 'Gracillimus'*)*, 33 (left), 88; **Peter
Loewer:** p. 45 *(Deschampsia
caespitosa* 'Fairy's Joke'*)*; **Julie
Maris-Semel:** p. 24; **Maggie
Oster:** pp. 9, 19, 21; **Carole
Ottesen:** p. 26; **Jerry Pavia:** pp.
15, 30 *(Equisetum hyemale)*,
36 (left), 73, 75, 77; **Joanne
Pavia:** p. 53; **Susan Roth:** pp.
16, 32, 51 (center), 55 (right);
Steven Still: pp. 20, 28, 29, 45
(Molinia caerulea 'Variegata'*)*,
51 (top), 86; **Michael S.
Thompson:** pp. 7, 31, 44 (left),
45 *(Pennisetum alopecuroides*
'Moudry'*)*, 47 (bottom);
Cynthia Woodyard: pp. 27
(top), 35, 38, 54, 55 (left).

Step-by-step photography by
Derek Fell.

Front cover photograph copyright © 1995 by Derek Fell.

All plant encyclopedia photog-
raphy is copyright © 1995 by
Derek Fell, except the follow-
ing, which are copyright ©
1995 by the individual photog-
raphers. **Karen Bussolini:**
Miscanthus sinensis var. *con-
densatus* 'Silberpfeil'; **David
Cavagnaro:** *Andropogon ger-
ardii, Miscanthus sinensis*
'Silberfeder'; **Rick Darke:**
*Andropogon virginicus,
Eragrostis spectabilis, Koeleria
cristata, Uniola paniculata,
Zizania aquatica;* **Saxon Holt:**
Buchloe dactyloides; **Carole
Ottesen:** *Elymus condensatus,
Erianthus ravennae;* **Jerry
Pavia:** *Acorus americanus;*
Susan Roth: *Bouteloua gracilis,
Milium effusum* 'Aureum';
Steven Still: *Carex pendula,
Festuca ovina* var. *glauca,
Phalaris canariensis,
Schizachyrium scoparium,
Scirpus tabernaemontani* var.
*zebrinus, Stipa calamagrostis,
Typha latifolia;* **Joseph
Strauch, Jr.:** *Molinia caerulea*
var. *arundinacea;* **Michael S.
Thompson:** *Oryzopsis
hymenoides, Stenotaphrum
secundatum* 'Variegatum';
Cynthia Woodyard: *Cordyline
australis.*